Negativity Neutralized: A Guide to Handling Difficult People

Navigating Challenging Relationships with Grace

Jennifer Scott

Table of Contents

INTRODUCTION

In life, we will definitely come with challenging individuals in all areas. Dealing with negative people and challenging behaviors —whether they are coworkers, family, friends, or even complete strangers—is an inevitable aspect of being human. These interactions can be upsetting, exhausting, and frequently leave us feeling helpless. "Negativity Neutralized: A Guide to Handling Difficult People - Navigating Challenging Relationships with Grace" is here to transform how you approach these interactions.

This book is a thorough guidebook created to provide you with the skills and techniques required to deal with challenging people confidently and gracefully; it is not just another self-help book. By comprehending the underlying reasons behind negativity and cultivating a more profound awareness of your reactions, you can transform difficult relationships into opportunities for personal development and empowerment.

You will learn about the characteristics of negativity and how it affects the person who is displaying it and those around them in the following pages. You'll learn how to prepare yourself mentally and emotionally, ensuring you remain composed and resilient in adversity. Effective communication is vital, and this book offers practical techniques to engage with difficult individuals constructively, without compromising your own well-being.

It's essential to set and uphold boundaries, and we'll walk you through the process of defining specific restrictions that safeguard your mental and emotional well-being. Additionally, you'll learn specific techniques for handling a variety of challenging personalities, such as narcissists, bullies, chronic complainers, and passive-aggressive individuals.

You may cultivate happier, more fulfilling relationships in all spheres of your life by putting in place long-term tactics for positive maintenance and creating a strong support system. You'll learn how to apply these concepts in real-world circumstances, so you'll always be ready for anything.

As you go out on this path, never forget that every challenging conversation presents an opportunity for personal development. "Negativity Neutralized" will empower you to navigate challenging relationships with grace, turning potential conflicts into harmonious connections.

CHAPTER I

Understanding Negativity

Defining Negativity

Because of its complexity, negativity can be a difficult notion to describe. It can take many different forms, ranging from sporadic episodes of pessimism to ingrained habits that affect the person and those around them. To effectively manage negativity in people, particularly in the context of interpersonal relationships, one must clearly understand what negativity in people is. This section delves into negativity's meaning, causes, and manifestations, offering a thorough grasp of this intricate phenomenon.

Fundamentally, negativity can be defined as a tendency toward pessimism and negative thought patterns. It frequently entails focusing more on the negative elements of circumstances than the upsides, dangers, and probable failures. Negative people typically expect the worst, voice concerns about encouraging advances, and predict unpleasant consequences. This perspective impacts how they see the world and how they interact with others, which can have a knock-on effect that lowers the spirits and reduces optimism in people around them.

Negativity has many different and complex sources. According to psychological theories, early life experiences such as upbringing and environmental influences might give rise to negativity. Youngsters raised in homes where criticism and pessimism are common may absorb these viewpoints and continue them into adulthood. Trauma and unfavorable life experiences can also promote unfavorable thought patterns, which heightens feelings of vulnerability and mistrust. Genetic predispositions also come into play, since certain people's neurological composition may make them more susceptible to negative thinking.

The cognitive, affective, and behavioral aspects of negativity can be further comprehended. Cognitively, negativity is characterized by skewed thought processes including filtering —where a person only considers the negative while disregarding the positive—and catastrophizing—where a person imagines the worst case scenario. These mental trajectories sustain a vicious cycle of pessimism, making overcoming their negative mindset challenging.

Negativity emotionally takes the form of persistent unhappiness, worry, and impatience. People that are negative frequently feel uncomfortable and unhappy all the time, which can result in mood disorders like anxiety and depression. Their continual negativity can be taxing for people around them, which has an effect on their relationships in addition to their well-being.

Negativity manifests behaviorally as a tendency to criticize or complain as well as acts and attitudes that lack excitement. Negative people can be quick to identify weaknesses and faults in other people as well as in themselves. This conduct can produce a poisonous atmosphere that breeds hatred and strife in both interpersonal and professional contexts. Furthermore, negative people may also exhibit reluctance to change because negative people are more inclined to fear the unfamiliar and prefer to stay in their comfort zones—even if it means missing out on possibilities for growth and improvement.

In social situations, negativity frequently shows itself more clearly. Those who are negative often find it difficult to establish and sustain positive connections because they tend to see only the bad in other people. They may talk, assign blame for their issues, and show a general lack of compassion. By isolating individuals from their peers, this conduct might cause social isolation and strengthen their pessimistic outlook.

The effects of negativity on mental and physical health are also significant. Prolonged negative thinking and the stress it causes can cause a host of health problems, including as immune system weakness, cardiovascular disease, and digestive disorders. There is ample evidence to support the mind-body connection, and living in constant negativity can seriously compromise one's general health and well-being.

To combat negativity, a complex strategy including behavioral, emotional, and cognitive therapies is needed. Negative thought patterns can be effectively challenged and altered with the help of cognitive-behavioral therapy (CBT). People can learn to recognize cognitive distortions and cultivate more wholesome, well-rounded thought patterns through CBT. Practices like mindfulness and meditation can also assist people in becoming more conscious of their negative feelings and thoughts, which will help them better control these experiences.

Developing emotional intelligence might be advantageous on an emotional level. These learning abilities can help people better understand and control their emotions, like empathy, self-awareness, and self-regulation. Developing emotional resilience is also essential because it helps people deal with hardship more positively.

Promoting constructive routines and actions might operate as a behavioral counterbalance to negativity. People's moods and perspectives on life can be improved by encouraging them to partake in enjoyable and fulfilling activities including hobbies, social contacts, and physical exercise. Positive experiences and appreciation exercises can also aid in removing the emphasis from negativity.

Creating a supportive environment that promotes positive relationships and discourages negative behaviors is one way to manage negativity in social environments. This can be accomplished by encouraging an environment of respect and gratitude, establishing clear limits, and maintaining open lines of communication. A more peaceful and productive atmosphere can be created by encouraging positive social standards and assisting those dealing with negativity.

In conclusion, negativity in humans is a complicated and multidimensional phenomenon with behavioral, emotional, and cognitive components. It can come from a variety of places, such as traumatic experiences, early life events, and inherited tendencies. Negativity affects the person as well as their relationships when it shows itself as skewed thought patterns, persistent discontent, and critical behaviors. A comprehensive strategy that incorporates emotional intelligence development, cognitive-behavioral therapies, and encouraging good social surroundings and habits is needed to combat negativity. To cultivate more satisfying and positive relationships and ultimately improve general well-being, it is necessary to recognize and address the underlying causes and expressions of negativity.

Sources of Negativity

Negativity is a pervasive and complex aspect of human behavior, influencing thoughts, emotions, and interactions. Effectively addressing negativity requires an understanding of its sources. These sources can be broadly divided into two categories: internal and external forces. Internal elements are those that come from within the person and include physiological, psychological, and emotional aspects. Conversely, external variables include relationships, cultural pressures, life experiences, and other aspects of the environment and social context. This section explores the intricate interplay between internal and external sources of negativity, providing a comprehensive understanding of their origins and impacts.

Internal sources of negativity are deeply rooted within an individual's psyche. A major contributing aspect is psychological, with cognitive distortions serving as the main culprit. Irrational, exaggerated thought patterns known as cognitive distortions are what feed negative thinking. Examples include all-or-nothing thinking, in which circumstances are seen in stark terms without considering the nuances, and catastrophizing, in which a person predicts the worst possible conclusion. These false beliefs can result in a chronically pessimistic mindset, which makes it difficult for people to see the positive parts of their lives.

Emotional variables also influence internal negativity. Individuals who suffer from long-term stress, anxiety, or depression are more prone to hold negative attitudes and thoughts. These emotional states have the potential to produce a negative feedback loop, in which unfavorable feelings feed unfavorable thought processes, creating a vicious cycle of negativity that is hard to escape. In addition, mental negativity can be fueled by low self-worth and self-esteem. Self-doubt and self-criticism are more common in those who lack confidence in their skills and abilities, which can intensify negative thinking.

It is impossible to ignore physiological aspects while thinking about internal sources of negativity. Depression symptoms and bad moods can be influenced by neurochemical imbalances in the brain, such as low serotonin and dopamine levels. Hormonal fluctuations, medical disorders, or genetic predispositions can all cause these abnormalities. For example, people with thyroid problems or long-term illnesses frequently feel more pessimistic because of the psychological and physical effects of their conditions. Lack of sleep and unhealthy eating habits also affect how the brain works and how emotions are regulated, which makes people more negative.

On the other hand, external stimuli and the surroundings are the causes of external negativity. Social connections are an essential outside factor. Be it with friends, family, or coworkers, toxic relationships may be a significant source of negativity. Persistent exposure to conflict, criticism, or emotional manipulation can weaken one's feeling of well-being and result in a pessimistic perspective. Moreover, emotions of negativity and inadequacy can be stoked by social comparison, which is driven by social media and cultural expectations. Constantly comparing oneself to others and feeling inadequate can cause people to be unhappy and have a poor opinion of themselves.

Events and situations in life can add to the negativity that comes from the outside. Traumatic events can have long-lasting detrimental effects on a person's mental and emotional health. Examples include losing a loved one, going through financial difficulties, or being the victim of abuse. These things can set off stress reactions and result in protracted depressive episodes. Furthermore, persistently stressful circumstances such as unstable employment, long-term illness, or trouble in relationships can produce a persistently negative atmosphere that impacts a person's perspective on life in general.

Strong external sources of negativity include cultural norms and societal forces. There is a significant emphasis on achievement, success, and adhering to standards in many cultures. People who feel they can't live up to these expectations could go through a lot of stress and unhappiness. The media, which usually presents idealized lives that are out of reach for most people, frequently exacerbates this. Anxiety to live up to these expectations might result in negative, inadequate, and insufficient sentiments.

There is a complicated and reciprocal interaction between negative internal and external forces. Internal factors might amplify the effects of external stressors. Anxious people, for example, may find it harder to handle outside demands, such as stress from the workplace, which can exacerbate their negative emotions. On the other hand, outside influences may make internal negativity worse. While a poisonous atmosphere might exacerbate internal negative thought patterns, a supportive and upbeat setting can lessen their impact.

Effectively combating negativity necessitates a comprehensive strategy that considers both internal and external factors. Cognitive-behavioral therapy (CBT) is a popular intervention for internal variables that assists people in recognizing and altering faulty thought habits. CBT promotes the growth of more positive, well-rounded thought patterns that might lessen internal negativity. People who use emotional regulation techniques like stress management and mindfulness can also better control their emotions.

Medications and lifestyle modifications are examples of physiological interventions that might be required to correct neurochemical imbalances and enhance brain function in general. Getting enough sleep, eating well, and exercising regularly can all help to lower internal negativity. People can also develop a more positive self-image through realistic goal-setting and the use of positive affirmations to boost self-esteem.

Building wholesome relationships is essential for mitigating the effects of outside negativity. This entails establishing boundaries with harmful people and looking for encouraging and constructive interactions. Building robust social networks can give people the emotional resources they need to handle challenges from the outside world. Negative external variables can also be lessened by controlling external stress through efficient time management, problem-solving techniques, and seeking expert assistance when necessary.

In conclusion, negativity arises from a complex interplay of internal and external factors. Internal factors, such as emotional emotions, physiological conditions, and cognitive distortions greatly influence an individual's negative view. Outside factors like negative relationships, significant life events, and social pressures also play essential roles. It is crucial to comprehend these sources and how they interact to combat negativity effectively. By implementing a comprehensive strategy that attends to both internal and external elements, people can mitigate negativity and foster a more optimistic and satisfying existence.

The Psychological Impact

Negativity is a ubiquitous and frequently subtle force that significantly affects the one displaying it and others around them. Negativity has psychological impacts that go far beyond temporary discomfort; they affect relationships, mental health, and general well-being. This section explores the complex psychological implications of negativity, looking at how it affects both the person who is holding negative ideas and behaviors and the others around them.

The psychological cost of negativity can be very high for the one who displays it. Catastrophizing and all-or-nothing thinking are examples of persistently negative thought processes that can affect one's understanding of reality. People that suffer from this cognitive bias find it difficult to see the bright side of things, which leads to a feeling of helplessness and hopelessness. Over time, these negative thought patterns can become deeply ingrained, making breaking free from their grip challenging. Prolonged negativity frequently shows up as chronic stress, despair, and anxiety. A vicious cycle of negative feelings and ideas can be started by persistently expecting the worse and concentrating on issues rather than potential solutions.

Negativity carries a heavy emotional cost. People who constantly display negativity are frequently more easily agitated, frustrated, and angry. These feelings can be quite strong and hard to control, which might cause frequent emotional outbursts or retreat. People who experience ongoing emotional strain also experience mental exhaustion and become less able to cope with daily challenges. Emotional exhaustion may be a factor in a reduction in cognitive performance, impacting one's capacity for memory, focus, and decision-making. When people struggle to find happiness and fulfillment in their daily activities, their overall quality of life declines.

The effects of negativity on an individual's physiology are equally worrisome. Long-term elevated cortisol levels result from the body's stress response being triggered by persistently unfavorable emotions. Numerous detrimental health impacts, such as a compromised immune system, an increased risk of cardiovascular illnesses, and digestive issues, can result from this ongoing state of physiological stress. Chronic stress can also cause sleep abnormalities, which can make emotional and cognitive problems worse. The physical toll of negativity creates a vicious cycle where poor health contributes to negative emotions, which in turn worsen physical well-being.

Negativity has a psychological effect on people in connections with others in addition to the individual. Because they prefer to concentrate on their failings and imperfections, negative people frequently find it difficult to maintain healthy, happy relationships. Their gloomy and critical viewpoint can lead to friction and strain in relationships with friends, family, and coworkers. These unfavorable encounters can weaken closeness and trust over time, straining relationships and increasing social isolation. Because of the persistent negativity, loved ones may find it difficult to offer assistance and may feel frustrated, powerless, or resentful.

Negativity can also affect the feelings and actions of others who are close to the negative person. Peers might get demotivated and pessimistic when someone with a negative view is around, especially in social and professional contexts. This phenomenon, known as emotional contagion, occurs when people unconsciously mimic the emotions and behaviors of those around them. For instance, a pessimistic coworker's attitude might raise job discontent, lower productivity, and lower team morale in the workplace. Within familial environments, spouses and kids can internalize the bad attitudes and actions they witness, developing similar negative patterns in themselves.

The stress and emotional strain of interacting with a negative person exacerbates the psychological effects of negativity on others. Those who are close to someone who is always negative may experience higher levels of stress and anxiety as a result. They could have the impression that they are continually treading carefully to prevent setting off further unfavorable emotions. This hypervigilance and stress can cause emotional burnout, in which people feel exhausted and incapable of meeting their own emotional needs.

A comprehensive strategy that considers both the negative person and those impacted by their conduct is needed to address the psychological effects of negativity. Cognitive behavioral therapy, often known as CBT, might be very beneficial for the person displaying negativity. CBT assists people in substituting more positive and balanced thought patterns by identifying and questioning negative thought patterns. Furthermore, by increasing emotional awareness and management, mindfulness exercises might lessen the severity and occurrence of unfavorable emotional reactions. Developing resilience via stress-reduction methods like physical activity and relaxation techniques can help lessen the physiological impacts of persistent negativity.

It's crucial for people impacted by negative people to build coping mechanisms. Managing the consequences of the negativity can be achieved by establishing clear boundaries and having honest conversations about its effects. Get the emotional resources you need to handle the stress and emotional strain by reaching out to friends, family, or licensed counselors. A more optimistic perspective can also be supported and the negative influence can be offset by creating a supportive environment and encouraging pleasant relationships.

It is essential to foster a culture of positivity and support in both social and professional contexts. Managers and leaders must encourage open communication, identify and deal with negativity, and create a welcoming environment. Positive reinforcement and team-building exercises can assist in changing the emphasis from negativity to cooperation and support amongst one another.

In conclusion, the psychological impact of negativity is profound and far-reaching, affecting both the individual exhibiting negative behaviors and those around them. Negativity affects the person in ways such as altered thinking, emotional anguish, and physical health problems. For others, spreading negativity can lead to social isolation, emotional distress, and stress. A multimodal strategy, including support networks, positive environment creation, and cognitive and emotional interventions, is needed to combat negativity. Positive relationships can be fostered and individuals and communities can improve general well-being by realizing the psychological effects of negativity and taking steps to mitigate them.

CHAPTER II

Self-Awareness and Preparation

Self-Assessment

A key element of emotional intelligence and personal development is self-assessment. It entails a thorough and sincere analysis of one's own triggers and reactions—that is, the feelings and actions brought on by particular circumstances or stimuli. It is crucial to comprehend these facets of oneself to manage stress, enhance interpersonal connections, and promote overall well-being. This section examines the value of self-assessment, how to identify triggers and emotions, and the advantages of growing in self-awareness.

Identifying your personal triggers is the first step in the process of self-evaluation. Events or situations outside of oneself that set off an emotional reaction are known as triggers. They can involve particular events, persons, locations, or even memories, and they can differ greatly from person to person. For instance, a coworker's critical remark may cause someone to feel inadequate and defensive, but getting caught in traffic may cause someone else to get extremely irritated. Since identifying these triggers entails paying close attention to the instances in which you experience an abrupt shift in your emotional state, it calls for reflection and awareness.

Keeping a journal or diary where you record your daily experiences and the emotions they evoke can help you identify your triggers. Patterns will begin to show themselves if you record the precise moments that trigger intense emotional responses. As an example, you may see that some social situations or professional duties routinely make you feel anxious or stressed. By doing this, one can better recognize triggers and gain insight into the situations in which they arise.

Examining your responses to your triggers is the next stage after you've determined what they are. The instantaneous behavioral and emotional reactions that occur after a trigger are known as reactions. These can involve behaviors like retreating, quarreling, or looking for solace, as well as emotions like rage, grief, fear, or delight. It's essential to pay attention to your replies both during the situation and afterward in order to comprehend how you react. This introspection aids in identifying if your responses are beneficial or harmful to your relationships and general well-being.

Self-assessment of responses can be especially difficult since it necessitates a high level of openness and vulnerability. It entails recognizing the feelings you experience and the actions you take as a result. For instance, it's crucial to investigate the reasons behind your defensive and angry responses to criticism. Maybe it comes from a past experience of being unfairly assessed or a worry of not being good enough. You can start addressing your reactions more skillfully if you know the underlying causes.

There are several advantages to increasing your self-awareness through self-evaluation. Better emotional management is one of the main benefits. You can better control these reactions when you know what sets off your emotions and how you usually respond to them. Instead of being caught off guard by your emotions, you can anticipate and prepare for them. Using calming methods to help you control your emotions in the present, such as mindfulness or deep breathing, may be part of this preparation.

Better decision-making is also a result of increased self-awareness. You may choose your responses more wisely when you are aware of your emotional triggers and reactions. For example, you can decide ahead of time how to deal constructively with a circumstance if you know it will likely cause stress. This could entail putting up limits, asking for help, or adopting an alternative perspective on the matter. Being proactive instead of reactive will help you deal with difficult situations more skillfully and easily.

In social interactions, self-awareness promotes communication and empathy. Awareness of your triggers and reactions makes you more sensitive to other people's emotional experiences. Your encounters will be of higher quality due to your increased sensitivity and compassion in response to this empathy. Additionally, you may interact with people more honestly and openly when you are conscious of your emotional reactions. More clarity in expressing your wants and feelings can foster mutual understanding and trust in your relationships.

Furthermore, self-evaluation fosters resilience and personal development. You get better at overcoming hardship by often reflecting on your emotional triggers and reactions. You come to see obstacles as chances for development as opposed to dangers. This change in viewpoint strengthens your resilience, enabling you to recover from setbacks faster and with more vigor. This perseverance eventually leads to a more upbeat and confident attitude on life.

The development of an inquisitive and nonjudgmental mindset is essential for practicing self-assessment. Rather than judging or condemning your responses, go into the process with an open mind and the goal of bettering your understanding of yourself. Remember that everyone experiences emotional reactions and triggers; the objective is to regulate these responses in a positive and healthy way rather than completely eradicate them.

One of the most effective tools for increasing self-awareness is mindfulness meditation. You can learn to notice your thoughts and feelings without letting them control you through mindfulness practices. By putting some distance between the trigger and your response, this technique can help you have more control over how you react. Frequent mindfulness meditation will help you become more adept at remaining grounded and in the moment, even when confronted with intense emotional triggers.

The process of self-evaluation may also benefit from therapy or counseling. A qualified therapist can offer direction and encouragement while you investigate your triggers and responses. They can assist you in identifying more profound underlying problems and creating more efficient coping mechanisms for your emotions. Therapy offers a secure, accepting environment where you can process your feelings and better understand who you are.

In conclusion, self-assessment is vital for recognizing your triggers and reactions. You may improve your self-awareness and emotional control by knowing what triggers your emotions and how you usually react. This knowledge fosters resilience and personal growth while also enhancing relationships and decision-making. Techniques like mindfulness and therapy, along with approaching self-evaluation with curiosity and non- judgment, can make navigating your emotional landscape easier and more successful. Through this process, you can better understand yourself and cultivate a more balanced and fulfilling life.

Mindset and Attitude

One's quality of life is greatly improved by the transforming process of developing a resilient and optimistic mindset. Attitude, a fixed way of thinking or feeling about something, and mindset, the predetermined set of attitudes an individual possesses, are related. They influence each other's perceptions of and reactions to our environment. A resilient and optimistic mindset involves more than just keeping an upbeat attitude; it also entails building the mental fortitude necessary to overcome obstacles in life. This section examines the value of developing this kind of thinking, the ideas that underpin it, and doable tactics for encouraging resilience and positivity.

One cannot stress the importance of having a resilient and optimistic mindset. According to psychology and neuroscience research, positive thinking has been repeatedly linked to improved mental and physical health, healthier relationships, and higher levels of overall life satisfaction. People with a resilient mindset are better able to handle hardship, bounce back from failures, and even prosper when faced with obstacles. It is the foundation of emotional well-being, allowing individuals to hold onto stability and direction in the face of life's unavoidable ups and downs.

The concept of growth versus fixed mindset is at the heart of cultivating a positive and resilient mindset, introduced by psychologist Carol Dweck. The idea that intelligence and skill are unchangeable, immutable attributes is known as a fixed mindset. This way of looking at things might cause dread of failing and a propensity to shy away from problems. On the other hand, a growth mentality is the conviction that commitment and diligence can enhance aptitude and intelligence. This kind of thinking encourages a passion for learning, fortitude in the face of adversity, and a stronger eagerness to take on new tasks.

Self-awareness is one of the cornerstones of a resilient and optimistic mindset. This entails understanding how one's ideas, feelings, and actions affect one's perspective on life and comprehending them. Self-awareness enables people to recognize harmful thought patterns and swap them out for more beneficial ones. For example, someone with a resilient and positive mindset can regard a setback as a chance for learning and progress rather than as a personal failure. This change in viewpoint can greatly lower stress and boost motivation.

The practice of gratitude is another important component. To be grateful is to acknowledge and value all of life's blessings, no matter how minor. Consistent thankfulness practice has been demonstrated to improve mood, lower stress levels, and enhance general well-being. It promotes focusing on what is good rather than what is wrong, which can assist in changing a person's perspective from one that is negative to one that is positive. Writing down one's blessings every day in a gratitude diary is a straightforward yet effective habit that can promote a more optimistic mindset.

Developing an optimistic and resilient mentality also requires the practice of mindfulness and meditation. Being mindful entails focusing on the here and now without passing judgment. By increasing one's awareness of one's thoughts and emotions, this practice enables people to react to circumstances more calmly and clearly. Specifically, it has been demonstrated that meditation lowers stress, improves emotional regulation, and raises emotions of well-being. People can increase their resilience and sense of inner calm by making mindfulness and meditation a regular part of their daily activities.

Thinking positively is another essential element. This is about concentrating on the possibilities for successful results and solutions rather than denying reality or acting as though everything is flawless. It entails changing pessimistic ideas to more optimistic ones. For instance, a person can reframe the idea to something like, "This is challenging, but I can learn and improve," instead of, "I can't do this." Rephrasing things in this way can increase self-assurance and lessen hopelessness.

A happy and resilient attitude also requires creating and sustaining strong social ties. Supportive relationships offer a sense of community, practical assistance, and emotional support. They can relieve stress and speed up people's recovery from setbacks. Participating in community events, preserving strong relationships with loved ones, and making new social contacts can all help cultivate a more optimistic and resilient perspective.

Another crucial tactic is to set objectives that are both attainable and reasonable. Objectives provide people with focus and direction, inspiring them to act and persevere in facing difficulties. Make sure your goals are time-bound, relevant, measurable, attainable, and specific (SMART) when you set them. Larger objectives can be made less intimidating and more reachable by breaking them down into smaller, more doable steps. This promotes a sense of progress and accomplishment.

Mental and emotional health are also significantly influenced by physical health. A balanced diet, regular exercise, and enough sleep are essential for preserving mental and emotional well-being. Particularly, exercise has been demonstrated to lessen anxiety and depressive symptoms, elevate mood, and improve cognitive performance. Taking good care of oneself can greatly impact one's mental health and foster a resilient and upbeat outlook.

Ultimately, it's critical to cultivate a feeling of meaning and purpose in life. This entails partaking in pursuits that are consistent with one's beliefs and interests. Having a purpose in life, whether it be through employment, interests, volunteer work, or relationships, gives one drive and a reason to stick with something when things become tough. It lets people look past their current problems and concentrate on their long-term objectives.

In conclusion, cultivating a positive and resilient mindset is a multifaceted process that involves self-awareness, gratitude, mindfulness, positive thinking, strong social connections, realistic goal-setting, physical well-being, and a sense of purpose. Through proactive efforts in these domains, people can cultivate the mental resilience required to handle life's obstacles and sustain an optimistic perspective effectively. Such a mindset positively affects all facets of life, including relationships, general well-being, and the development of a stronger sense of contentment and fulfillment. Anyone can develop a resilient and optimistic mindset through commitment and practice, which will change how they approach life and how they see it.

Emotional Intelligence

The ability to identify, comprehend, regulate, and influence one's emotions and those of others is known as emotional intelligence, or EQ for short. It includes various abilities essential for good interpersonal relations, communication, and personal well-being. The two main facets of emotional intelligence are self-control and empathy. These components are crucial to connecting with the environment, controlling their emotions, and preserving wholesome relationships. This section delves into the significance of empathy and self-control within the emotional intelligence framework, highlighting their enormous influence on individual and occupational achievement.

The capacity to comprehend and experience another person's emotions is known as empathy. It entails being aware of emotional signs, understanding the underlying feelings, and reacting kind and encouragingly. Since empathy fosters stronger connections and improves interpersonal relationships, it is a fundamental component of emotional intelligence. Empathetic people can better establish rapport, settle disputes, and promote a positive atmosphere. People with empathy can put themselves in other people's shoes, view their experiences from their point of view, and react accordingly.

Empathy promotes closeness and comprehension in interpersonal interactions. It makes it possible for people to emotionally connect at a deeper level, which is crucial for creating solid, enduring relationships. When family members, friends, or lovers show empathy for one another, they establish a secure environment in which emotions and experiences can be shared. This shared understanding builds bridges between people and serves as the basis for productive dialogue and problem-solving. An understanding reaction, for instance, can reassure and comfort a buddy going through a trying moment by making them feel acknowledged and important.

Empathy is just as vital in work environments. Empathic managers and leaders can better comprehend their staff's wants and needs. Employees feel appreciated and supported in a great work environment that is fostered by this understanding. Since they can adjust their strategy to fit their staff's emotional and psychological demands, empathic leaders are better at inspiring their groups. Furthermore, empathy is essential to customer service, as recognizing and attending to clients' emotions can increase their pleasure and loyalty.

Another essential element of emotional intelligence is self-regulation, which is controlling one's own emotions, especially under pressure or in difficult circumstances. It necessitates the capacity to remain composed, concentrated, and composed in the face of difficulty. Making logical decisions and preserving emotional equilibrium need self-regulation. It makes it possible for people to react to circumstances thoughtfully and constructively rather than impulsively.

Self-control is especially crucial when resolving conflicts. Emotionally stable people are better equipped to have constructive conversations and create win-win solutions when conflicts emerge. They can approach the situation with a calm and open perspective, which helps to de-escalate emotions and promote cooperation, as opposed to reacting defensively or aggressively. Regulating emotions is essential for healthy interactions and more efficient problem-solving in personal and professional relationships.

Furthermore, self-control enhances mental health in general. People can lessen stress and avoid emotional exhaustion by controlling their negative emotions, such as anger, impatience, or anxiety. Effective methods for improving self-regulation include cognitive reframing, deep breathing, and mindfulness. For example, practicing mindfulness, which focuses on the here and now without judgment, can make people more conscious of their emotions and enable them to react more carefully. Exercises involving deep breathing can help soothe the nervous system and lessen the adverse physiological effects of stress. Cognitive reframing is a technique that modifies one's perspective on a situation to encourage a more positive outlook and disrupt negative thought processes.

Self-regulation and empathy must work together to build and preserve emotional intelligence. Emotional overload can result from empathy without self-control because people may become too consumed with other people's feelings and lose sight of their own emotional equilibrium. On the other hand, emotional detachment—the state in which people successfully control their own emotions but cannot relate to others—can arise from self-regulation in the absence of empathy. Therefore, cultivating wholesome, supportive relationships and achieving emotional well-being require striking a balance between empathy and self-regulation.

Empathy and self-control together can improve organizational success and leadership effectiveness in the workplace. Leaders who possess empathy and emotional self-control are more adept at handling the intricacies of interpersonal relationships and fostering a healthy work atmosphere. They are able to effectively manage team dynamics, encourage trust and loyalty among their staff, and handle sensitive and awkward topics. This set of abilities is especially crucial at times of crisis or transition, as the capacity to maintain composure and empathy can aid in guiding the company through difficulties.

Developing emotional intelligence, especially empathy and self-regulation, takes deliberate practice and introspection. People can improve their empathy by actively listening to others, attempting to comprehend their viewpoints, and demonstrating sincere concern for their well-being. People can learn the skills necessary to effectively manage their emotional states and increase their awareness of them by engaging in mindfulness practices and other self-regulation exercises. Getting input from others and participating in ongoing education can also give one important insights into their emotional intelligence and places for development.

In conclusion, empathy and self-regulation are fundamental components of emotional intelligence that significantly impact personal and professional success. Self-regulation helps people control their emotions, keep emotional equilibrium, and make logical decisions, while empathy improves interpersonal interactions by promoting understanding, trust, and compassion. The interaction of these abilities is necessary for the growth and maintenance of emotional intelligence, which promotes better relationships, greater well-being, and more capable leadership. People can successfully negotiate the complexity of human emotions, forge closer bonds with others, and succeed more broadly in all facets of life by developing empathy and self-regulation.

CHAPTER III

Communication Strategies

Active Listening

A vital communication ability, active listening entails more than just hearing what is being said; it also entails giving the speaker your whole attention, comprehending what they are saying, and deliberately answering. This ability is crucial for establishing trusting bonds, settling disputes, and encouraging a greater understanding among people. In a time when real connections can be hard to find, and distractions abound, developing the skill of active listening can significantly improve relationships in both personal and professional spheres. This section examines the value of active listening, its methods, and its advantages for relationships and communication.

Making a conscious effort to hear not just what is being said, but also the feelings and intentions that are being conveyed, is necessary for active listening. The speaker feels appreciated and understood when they are engaged to this degree since it shows empathy and respect. Active listening has many advantages, one of which is that it fosters rapport and trust. People are more inclined to open up and express their thoughts and feelings in important and fruitful conversations when they feel like they are being truly heard.

Keeping eye contact is one of the most essential active listening strategies. Making eye contact lets the speaker know you are paying attention and finding their words interesting. It demonstrates your whole presence in the conversation and aids in building a relationship. Overly intense eye contact can be unsettling, therefore, it's crucial to make sure that it feels natural and unforced when maintaining eye contact. Maintaining eye contact while taking brief breaks to look away can help to keep the exchange comfortable.

Nonverbal feedback is an essential component of active listening. You can do this by nodding, grinning, and making facial gestures that convey your interest and comprehension. Nonverbal cues are effective ways to show empathy and focus. They demonstrate your active processing of their message and your reaction to their feelings to the speaker. Building rapport and fostering a sense of understanding between the parties can also be achieved by gently mirroring the speaker's body language.

Restating what the speaker has said in your own words is known as paraphrasing. This allows the speaker to address any misunderstandings and shows that you have accurately received what they are saying. For instance, you might say, "So, you're feeling overwhelmed by the workload and frustrated with the lack of support from your team?" in response to a friend talking about a difficult situation at work. In addition to demonstrating that you are paying attention, paraphrasing pushes the other person to go farther into their ideas and emotions.

Reflective listening goes beyond simple paraphrase to include recognizing the speaker's feelings. To ensure accuracy, you must identify the feelings you detect and follow up with the speaker. Say, "It sounds like you're really stressed and disappointed with how things are going at work," as an example. Reflective listening allows the speaker to expound on their experience while also helping to affirm their feelings. This method exhibits empathy and encourages a stronger emotional bond.

Another critical tactic in active listening is to pose open-ended inquiries. Rather than offering a straightforward yes or no response, these questions compel the speaker to elaborate on their ideas and emotions. Typically, open-ended queries start with "how," "what," or "why." For example, you may ask, "How did that situation make you feel?" instead of, "Are you upset about what happened?" This gives the audience a deeper grasp of the speaker's perspective and encourages them to share additional information.

One part of active listening that is sometimes missed is silence. Encouraging pauses in the discourse allows the speaker to gather their thoughts. It also demonstrates your patience and willingness to provide them the room to express themselves completely. Silence can be very effective when discussing sensitive subjects since it gives the speaker time to collect their ideas and feelings without feeling pressed for time.

Condensing the essential ideas of the discussion and bringing them back to the speaker is the process of summarizing. This supports and validates your comprehension of the main ideas covered in the conversation. Saying something like, "So, to summarize, you're concerned about the timeline and you feel that we need more resources to meet the deadline," could be used to wrap up a discussion about a project at work. By providing a clear framework for future action, summarizing ensures that all stakeholders are on the same page.

The foundation of active listening is empathy. It entails placing oneself in the speaker's position and attempting to comprehend their viewpoint and emotions. To be empathetic, one must pay attention to nonverbal indicators given by the speaker, such as body language, tone of voice, and facial expressions. Empathy-based communication can strengthen bonds between people and promote mutual respect and trust.

Remaining focused on the speaker and controlling distractions are other aspects of active listening. It's simple to get sidetracked in today's fast-paced world by multitasking, technology, or other outside influences. But for active listening to be genuinely effective, you must give the speaker your whole attention. This may be putting your phone away, finding a quiet space to speak, and mentally putting any other work or worries on hold. You can convey to the speaker that their message is significant and deserving of your attention by giving them your whole attention.

Active listening has several advantages that go well beyond the current discussion. It can result in better communication, more profound comprehension, and more efficient problem-solving. Active listening makes partners feel heard and validated, which fosters closeness and trust in interpersonal interactions. It can improve collaboration, teamwork, and dispute resolution in work environments. Organizations may enhance productivity, raise morale, and improve communication by cultivating an environment that values active listening.

In conclusion, active listening is a vital skill that involves fully engaging with the speaker, understanding their message, and responding thoughtfully. Active listening consists of various skills, including keeping eye contact, giving nonverbal cues, paraphrasing, reflecting, asking open-ended questions, allowing for silence, summarizing, and exhibiting empathy. People can strengthen their connections, promote more understanding, and improve their general communication skills by learning these strategies and maintaining their attention on the speaker. Active listening lays the groundwork for meaningful and productive encounters by fostering a deeper connection with the person you are listening to than just hearing what they say.

Assertiveness vs. Aggressiveness

Communicating clearly and assertively is crucial for setting boundaries and voicing demands and opinions in both personal and professional contexts. Nonetheless, there's frequently a misunderstanding between aggressive and forceful behavior. While advocating for oneself is a part of both actions, their methods and outcomes are very different. Aggression is about controlling or disregarding others, whereas assertiveness is about expressing oneself with confidence and deference. The differences between aggressiveness and assertiveness, the significance of striking a balance between firmness and respect, and techniques for honing assertive communication skills are all covered in this section.

A straightforward, honest, and respectful communication to both the speaker and the listener is a hallmark of assertiveness. It entails speaking up confidently and thoughtfully while expressing needs, feelings, and views. An assertive individual strikes a balance between respect for oneself and others by expressing their viewpoint without disparaging or undermining others. This method facilitates open communication and cooperative problem-solving, which builds mutual understanding and positive connections.

Conversely, aggressiveness is characterized by a controlling and frequently antagonistic communication style. Aggressive people often use intimidation, compulsion, or manipulation to accomplish their objectives. They put their own demands and opinions ahead of those of others. This behavior disregards other people's feelings and rights, leading to conflict, resentment, and dread. Aggression, as opposed to assertiveness, damages relationships and can create a poisonous atmosphere that stifles candid and open discussion.

To separate assertiveness from aggression, one must strike a balance between respect and toughness. Being firm entails stating one's requirements and boundaries clearly and concisely while adhering to one's views and ideals. But respect makes sure that others' liberty and dignity are not sacrificed in the name of firmness. Effective communication requires this balance because it enables people to speak up for themselves without offending or alienating those around them.

Self-awareness is one of the cornerstones of aggressive communication. To properly articulate one's needs, feelings, and boundaries, one must first understand them. Knowing when to speak up and how to do it courteously and transparently are both aspects of self-awareness. It also requires being aware of the effects that one's words and deeds have on other people to maintain pleasant and productive communication.

Active listening is another essential component of assertiveness. Being assertive means being willing to listen to and comprehend others in addition to voicing one's own opinions. Effective communication is a two-way process. Active listening entails giving the speaker your undivided attention, respecting their point of view, and giving a considered response. This approach facilitates rapport-building and creates a cooperative environment where everyone feels heard and respected.

Assertive communication also requires the establishment and maintenance of limits. By defining what is appropriate and inappropriate behavior, boundaries assist people in safeguarding their wellbeing and preserving wholesome relationships. Those that are assertive express their boundaries in a straightforward manner and uphold them consistently—all without using force. An assertive approach, for instance, may be to say quietly, "I'd like to finish my point before you respond," as opposed to becoming irate or frustrated if a coworker keeps interrupting during meetings.

The ability to communicate nonverbally is crucial to assertiveness. Nonverbal cues like tone of voice, body language, and facial expressions can all reinforce or contradict spoken communication. Nonverbal cues, such as keeping eye contact, adopting an open, relaxed posture, and speaking in a clear, steady tone, are used by assertive people to support their messages. A good and authoritative presence can be established with the help of these cues, which convey confidence and respect.

Another area where assertiveness comes in very handy is conflict resolution. A direct and constructive approach to problem-solving in conflict or tense situations is provided by assertive communication. In order to discover solutions that both parties can agree upon, assertive people should concentrate on the issue at hand rather than making personal jabs. Aggression, on the other hand, tends to aggravate confrontations and foster greater resentment. This strategy stands in stark contrast to it.

Commitment and practice are necessary to build forceful communication abilities. Using "I" statements instead of "you" utterances is one such tactic. "I" statements emphasize communicating one's own wants and feelings without placing blame or criticism on other people. It is more aggressive and less confrontational to say something like, "I feel overwhelmed when tasks are added to my schedule without notice," instead of "You always dump extra work on me at the last minute." This change in wording facilitates politely and clearly expressing concerns.

Rehearsal and role-playing are also helpful in developing assertiveness. People can feel more confident and equipped to speak up in real-life situations by practicing assertive responses in various contexts. Asking mentors or close friends for their opinions might yield insightful information and help to strengthen constructive communication practices.

It's critical to understand that being assertive involves having polite, honest conversations rather than always getting one's way. Collaboration and compromise are frequently required, and assertive people are prepared to bargain and come up with solutions that consider all parties' requirements and viewpoints. As opposed to both passivity and hostility, assertiveness is willing to have a positive conversation.

In conclusion, assertiveness and aggressiveness are distinct communication styles with different impacts on relationships and interactions. In order to promote mutual understanding and wholesome relationships, assertiveness requires clear, straightforward, and courteous communication that strikes a balance between firmness and respect. Contrarily, aggression entails a harsh, controlling demeanor that puts one's wants ahead of others, resulting in hatred and conflict. Becoming an effective communicator takes practice, self-awareness, active listening, and boundary-setting. Adopting assertiveness enables people to effectively represent their interests while engaging in cordial and courteous relationships with others. Maintaining this equilibrium is crucial for individual and occupational accomplishments, as it facilitates positive and significant dialogue in all aspects of life.

De-escalation Techniques

De-escalation techniques are vital instruments for handling and defusing heated situations. These methods are intended to lessen the ferocity of disagreement, soothe feelings, and promote productive communication. Defusing tensions in a politicized and high-stress environment is more critical than ever. This section examines the value of de-escalation, different methods for reducing stress, and the advantages of developing these abilities in both personal and professional settings.

Avoiding confrontations from getting out of control or damaging is the main objective of de-escalation. Misunderstandings, intense feelings, or perceived dangers are frequently the root causes of tense situations. Anger, anxiety, or frustration can cloud rational thought when emotions are strong, resulting in behaviors that intensify the conflict. By lowering the emotional intensity, de-escalation tactics help everyone involved think more clearly and communicate effectively.

Active listening is one of the most basic de-escalation strategies. This entails paying close attention to the speaker, expressing empathy, and endorsing their viewpoint. The other person may feel heard and understood when you actively listen to them, which can greatly lessen their emotions' severity. Empathizing actions might help the other person relax, such as nodding, keeping eye contact, and paraphrasing what they've said. Saying something like, "I can tell you're really upset about this," "Let's talk about what happened," might be used to support them in feeling heard and to start a productive conversation.

Keeping a cool head and a collected expression is another crucial tactic. Since emotions may spread easily, being composed might also affect how someone else feels. This entails managing your own facial expressions, tone of speech, and body language. Maintaining an open and relaxed posture helps communicate that you are approachable and not a threat, while speaking in a calm, steady, and kind tone can assist calm the other person. It's critical to refrain from using defensive or violent body language, like clenching fists or crossing arms, to stop the situation from worsening.

A useful technique for de-escalation is empathy. You can address the underlying problems fueling the disagreement by trying to comprehend the other person's feelings and point of view. Saying something like, "I understand that this situation is frustrating for you," might demonstrate your empathy and willingness to work with them to find a solution. By fostering rapport and trust, empathy makes it simpler to identify points of agreement and defuse tense situations.

Another good de-escalation strategy is to establish boundaries that are courteous and unambiguous. Conflicts can often get out of hand when people think their boundaries are being crossed. You can avoid misunderstandings and ease tension by declaring your own boundaries calmly and unambiguously and respecting those of others. Saying something like, "I want to continue this discussion, but let's take a five-minute break to cool down first," could be used in a heated conversation. This takes action to control the situation while simultaneously demonstrating regard for the other person's sentiments.

A tense situation can also be defused by offering options and alternatives. People may get stressed and behave aggressively when they feel helpless or confined. By providing options, one can lessen emotions of powerlessness and regain control over their life. We can manage this in numerous ways, for example, if someone is upset about something at work. Let's consider your options and determine the most suitable for you. This cooperative method can assist in moving the emphasis from dispute resolution to problem-solving.

When appropriately employed, humor can be a helpful de-escalation technique. Jokes or lighthearted remarks can ease stress and foster a more laid-back environment. But be careful when using humor—it can backfire if the other person thinks you're not paying attention to their worries. When use comedy, it's essential to assess the circumstances and the other person's emotional state. Executing effectively can help break the ice and facilitate more fruitful dialogue.

When emotions become too strong for productive conversation, time-outs can be useful for defusing the situation. Everyone concerned can cool down and gather their thoughts by taking a pause. This can stop the dispute from getting worse and allow everyone involved to handle the matter more rationally. The purpose of the time-out should be made clear. For example, you may say, "Let's take a short break and come back to this conversation in ten minutes." This demonstrates your dedication to finding a solution while acknowledging when a break is necessary.

De-escalation can also be facilitated by using stress management and mindfulness practices. Exercises that promote mindfulness, including deep breathing, meditation, or grounding, can assist you in managing your own stress and keeping a composed demeanor. Being composed makes you more capable of managing tense situations and influencing other people's emotions. An atmosphere that is more calm and concentrated can also be produced by encouraging people to partake in these activities.

Beyond just resolving conflicts right away, learning de-escalation strategies has several advantages. These abilities support the development of trust and long-term relationships. People are more likely to feel safe and appreciated in your presence when they are aware of your ability to resolve disputes amicably and politely. Stronger relationships, increased transparency and honesty in communication, and a more cooperative atmosphere can result from this.

Professional environments greatly benefit from de-escalation abilities. They contribute to a positive corporate culture, strengthen team chemistry, and improve customer service. Workers are more likely to be engaged and motivated when they feel valued and heard, which boosts output and job satisfaction. De-escalation skills are essential for leaders to have to keep their teams cohesive and productive.

In conclusion, de-escalation techniques are essential for managing and diffusing tense situations. Effective de-escalation techniques include active listening, being composed, demonstrating empathy, setting limits, offering choices, utilizing humor sensibly, taking time-outs, and engaging in mindfulness exercises. These methods aid in fostering understanding, lessening the intensity of emotions, and facilitating productive conversation. Gaining proficiency in de-escalation techniques not only settles disputes quickly but also strengthens and fosters trust in interpersonal and professional settings. By implementing these strategies, people may skillfully resolve disputes, fostering a cooperative and calm atmosphere.

CHAPTER IV

Setting Boundaries

Importance of Boundaries

It is impossible to overestimate the significance of boundaries in preserving mental and emotional well-being. Boundaries are crucial restrictions people establish to specify appropriate conduct, safeguard personal space, and guarantee well-being. They act as rules for how we should behave both in social situations and when it comes to our own emotional and mental health. Healthy limits must be set and upheld to promote relationships, avoid burnout, and promote self-respect. This section examines the value of boundaries, their impact on mental and emotional well-being, and practical methods for establishing and upholding them.

Since boundaries serve to define personal limitations, they are essential for maintaining one's mental and emotional well-being. These boundaries make sure people don't go overboard or let other people in their personal space. Without boundaries, people could find themselves putting in excessive work, putting up with rude behavior, or putting their own needs last to appease others. Stress, anxiety, and a feeling of being overburdened may result from this. Establishing boundaries is a safeguard, enabling people to control their resources and preserve their mental and emotional health.

Preventing burnout is one of the main advantages of setting boundaries. Burnout is a condition of extreme physical, mental, and emotional tiredness brought on by extended periods of high stress. It frequently happens when people feel overburdened by their obligations and don't have the time or energy to unwind. People can more efficiently manage their time and energy by establishing limits, which guarantees that they have enough time for relaxation and self-care. A professional might, for instance, establish guidelines for their working hours, ensuring they never respond to emails or conduct business calls when they are on their own time. By balancing work and personal life, this division lowers the possibility of burnout.

Setting limits is also essential for promoting self-worth and self-respect. People convey to themselves and others that their wants and well-being are essential when establishing and upholding boundaries. This self-advocacy action strengthens one's sense of empowerment and self-worth. in the other hand, those who don't establish boundaries may feel as though their needs are constantly disregarded or underestimated, which can cause them to become resentful, frustrated, and low in self-esteem. People who establish boundaries uphold their autonomy to prioritize their own health and well-being.

Setting and upholding healthy boundaries is crucial to preserving and enhancing relationships. Each party knows the other's needs and limitations when relationships respect boundaries. Respect like this promotes communication, trust, and security. For example, in a romantic relationship, partners are more likely to feel understood and supported if they clearly discuss their boundaries regarding social activities, personal space, and time alone. Setting boundaries lets everyone know what is expected of them and what constitutes appropriate behavior, which helps to avoid miscommunication and conflict.

On the other hand, undefined boundaries can lead to toxic and destructive relationships. Without boundaries, there could be an unequal distribution of power and respect as one person attempts to control or dominate the other. This can lead to codependency, a condition in which one person overindulges in the other's emotional support and validation while ignoring their own needs. People build a foundation for balanced, healthy relationships where both sides can prosper by setting limits.

Establishing boundaries aids people in controlling their emotional reactions and safeguarding their mental well-being. Individuals who permit their boundaries to be crossed may feel more stressed, anxious, or distressed emotionally. For instance, a person who finds it difficult to say no might consent to accept more duties or responsibilities even when they are already overburdened. Anger, resentment, and dissatisfaction may result from this. People can avoid these kinds of circumstances and keep control over their mental health by establishing boundaries.

Understanding that establishing limits does not equate to being inflexible or stiff is critical. Instead, it is being open to compromise and negotiation while still being forthright and explicit about one's wants and boundaries. Personal beliefs and priorities should serve as the foundation for boundaries, which may need to be modified over time as conditions change. For instance, when a child gets older and more self-reliant, a parent might need to modify their boundaries. Boundary-setting flexibility promotes development and adaptability while safeguarding a person's mental and emotional well-being.

Setting boundaries effectively calls for communication abilities and self-awareness. People must first recognize their own needs, boundaries, and stressors. They can firmly and clearly state their boundaries since they are self-aware. Establishing and upholding boundaries requires respectfully and assertively expressing one's demands and limitations to others, which is why communication is so important. Saying something like, "I value our friendship, but I need some personal time to recharge," could be appropriate if a buddy constantly demands time from you. Instead, let's arrange to meet next week." By using this strategy, you respect the relationship and express your boundaries.

Setting limits can be difficult sometimes, particularly when people resist or push back. Maintaining one's limits in the face of opposition requires persistence and consistency. This could entail stating the limit again, asking for help, or, in certain situations, putting distance between oneself and people who routinely cross boundaries. If a coworker is getting in the way of your job, for instance, you may need to have an open discussion about how important it is to have uninterrupted attention and come up with a solution that respects your boundaries.

In conclusion, boundaries are critical for safeguarding emotional and mental well-being. They support interpersonal improvement, emotional regulation, self-respect and self-esteem, and the avoidance of burnout. It takes self-awareness, skillful communication, and a commitment to constantly enforcing limitations to set and maintain boundaries. Individuals can prioritize their needs and well-being and live a healthier, more balanced life by setting clear boundaries. Setting boundaries is about creating a respectful and safe space where oneself and others can flourish, not about excluding others. Establishing boundaries helps people feel more in charge of their life and more empowered, which improves their mental and emotional well-being in the long run.

How to Set Boundaries

Establishing good relationships, ensuring one's needs are satisfied, and preserving one's mental and emotional well-being all depend on setting boundaries. Boundaries serve as standards for appropriate conduct and aid in people's efficient use of their time, energy, and resources. Setting limits, though, can be difficult, particularly if you're not used to doing it. This section emphasizes the value of communication, consistency, and clarity while examining doable strategies and offering scripts for establishing boundaries in various spheres of life.

Being self-aware is the first step in establishing limits. Before expressing your needs, values, and boundaries to others, you must first understand them yourself. Think back on any circumstances that make you feel uneasy, anxious, or taken advantage of. These emotions frequently serve as warning signs when your boundaries are being violated. Finding these patterns and getting clarity on what limits need to be set can be accomplished with the aid of journaling.

Communicating your boundaries authoritatively and clearly is the next step after determining what they are. Setting and maintaining limits that are respected by others depends on effective communication. It's critical to communicate your demands using "I" words without coming across as judgmental. Rather than stating, "You never give me any space," for instance, you may add, "I need some alone time to recharge." By emphasizing your wants more than assigning blame, this strategy increases the likelihood that the other person will react favorably.

One of the most critical aspects of creating boundaries is learning how to say no. Saying no can be difficult for many people because they worry about upsetting others or coming across as conceited. But it's crucial to remember that putting your well-being first is a valid and essential component of saying no. Begin by practicing basic, courteous rejections. If a coworker asks you to take on more work than you can handle, for example, you could respond with something like, "I appreciate you thinking of me, but I am currently at capacity with my workload." This script firmly establishes a boundary while acknowledging the request.

To set limits in a relationship, there must be courteous and open communication. It's critical to set clear boundaries in relationships, whether they be with loved ones, close friends, or romantic partners, openly and thoughtfully. Saying something like, "I value our conversations, but I need to prioritize my sleep," might be used if a buddy keeps calling you late at night and interfering with your sleep. Can we agree to have a conversation before ten o'clock at night?" This script acknowledges the partnership and conveys your need for relaxation.

Setting limits at work is crucial for stress management and productivity maintenance. To avoid burnout, being transparent about your availability and workload is critical. Saying something like, "I am committed to meeting our deadlines, but I also need to maintain a healthy work-life balance," could be your response to your boss if they frequently ask you to remain late. Can we talk about how to handle the workload during business hours?" This strategy establishes a firm limit while displaying your commitment.

The emotional complexities involved in setting limits with family members can make the process particularly difficult. But to keep partnerships healthy, it's critical to convey your wants. You might reply, "I appreciate your concern, but I would prefer to keep my personal decisions private," if a family member regularly makes uninvited remarks about your personal life. This script politely states that you need autonomy. When setting limits, it's essential to be consistent. It is crucial to maintain your limits regularly after you have made them clear to prevent misunderstandings and guarantee that they are kept. Reiterate your boundaries and deal with anyone who crosses them right away. For instance, you could explain, "I've noticed that my items are not being returned," if a friend keeps taking things out without returning them. In the future, please ask before borrowing anything." In addition to immediately addressing the behavior, this strengthens the barrier.

It's also critical to understand that establishing boundaries could first result in reaction or opposition. This is particularly valid when establishing limits with individuals who frequently cross them. Maintaining your composure and assertiveness in the face of opposition is critical. Remind yourself that prioritizing your needs is acceptable and that setting boundaries is essential to self-care.

Setting and upholding limits might be aided by seeking assistance. Talk about your boundaries with family members, close friends, or a therapist who can support and guide you. Maintaining your limits is essential, and having a support system can help you stay accountable.

Another crucial component of establishing boundaries is flexibility. While it's critical to maintain your integrity, there may be instances in which you should modify your limits in light of evolving events or fresh facts. For example, you can consent to change your border for a predetermined amount of time as long as you ensure it is restored afterward if a work project necessitates temporary overtime. Having flexibility enables you to prioritize your entire well-being while remaining adaptable.

Finally, remember to be compassionate with yourself while you establish limits. When you voice your demands, especially if you're not used to doing so, it's normal to experience feelings of guilt or unease. Remind yourself that preserving your mental and emotional well-being requires the good habit of setting limits. Honor your accomplishments, no matter how minor, and understand that developing comfort in establishing and upholding boundaries requires time and effort.

In conclusion, setting boundaries is vital for protecting mental and emotional health, fostering healthy relationships, and ensuring that personal needs are met. Being able to say no, being consistent, communicating clearly, and being self-aware are all necessary for the process. People can effectively set and uphold limits in various life contexts by utilizing doable procedures and scripts. Setting boundaries has many advantages over the long run, even though it may be difficult at first. Setting boundaries can become a powerful and transformational part of one's own development and well-being with practice and self-compassion.

Enforcing Boundaries

Setting and upholding boundaries is essential to preserving one's mental and emotional health since it guarantees that one's needs, boundaries, and personal space are honored. While establishing boundaries is crucial, maintaining them consistently and guilt-free can often be the true problem. This section looks at the need of setting limits, practical methods for doing so, and ways to deal with and get past guilt feelings related to setting boundaries.

Setting and upholding limits is crucial to retaining one's dignity and wholesome relationships. People set boundaries and safeguard their wellbeing by expressing their limitations and expectations to others. But if these limits are not upheld, they become ineffective and may cause feelings of bitterness, annoyance, and exhaustion. Setting and upholding boundaries on a regular basis guarantees that people respect and are aware of your requirements, laying the groundwork for positive relationships and respect for one another.

People often find it difficult to set limits because they are afraid of looking bad. A common source of guilt is fear of upsetting other people, coming across as conceited, or starting a fight. This dread may be especially strong in people who are used to putting other people's needs ahead of their own. It's crucial to understand, though, that setting and upholding limits is a necessary self-care activity rather than a selfish one. You can help and interact with people in a healthy and sustainable way if you put your health first.

Expressing boundaries firmly and explicitly is essential if you want to enforce them. Being direct, courteous, and non-aggressive while communicating your demands and boundaries is a key component of assertive communication. One way to respond to someone asking you to take on more work than you can do is to say, "I appreciate your confidence in my abilities, but I am currently at full capacity with my workload." I'm not able to take on any more work right now." This sentence conveys your boundaries clearly and professionally.

It's important to enforce limits consistently. Maintaining a boundary once you've set one is crucial to avoiding giving conflicting messages. Being inconsistent can make people doubt your boundaries and encourage recurrent boundary crossings. It's vital to constantly follow whatever boundaries you may have set, like avoiding returning work-related emails after a specific hour. If you reply to emails after this window of time, you risk undermining the barrier and creating the impression that you are always available.

Anticipating and becoming ready for possible backlash is another useful tactic for setting limits. Individuals who are used to specific behaviors could try to push your boundaries and reject changes. Even when you encounter resistance, it's critical to maintain your resolve and self-assurance in your boundaries. Do not allow guilt or coercion to influence you when you assertively and calmly reaffirm your boundaries. Say, "I understand that you need help, but I am unable to assist you at this time," in response to a friend who keeps asking you for favors at inconvenient times. Next time, please let me know in advance, and I'll try to be of assistance."

Setting limits and managing guilt are two important things. When you voice your demands, especially if you're not used to doing so, it's normal to experience some degree of guilt. But it's crucial to question and reinterpret these emotions. Remind yourself that preserving your well-being requires you to establish and enforce boundaries. Think about the long-term advantages of setting limits, such lowered stress levels, strengthened bonds with others, and more self-respect. Realize that by looking for yourself, you can engage with people more effectively and with greater presence.

Getting assistance from a therapist, family member, or trusted friend can also be beneficial for controlling guilt and reiterating boundaries. Talking to supportive people about your boundaries and any guilt you may have related with them can help to validate and uplift you. They can provide viewpoints that reaffirm the significance of boundaries and support your continued commitment to maintaining them. A therapist's expert assistance can also offer techniques for controlling guilt and developing assertiveness.

Another crucial factor to consider is the enforcement of boundaries with flexibility. Even while consistency is crucial, there can be instances in which changing your boundaries in light of particular situations is appropriate. Being flexible enables you to put your general well-being first while adjusting to new circumstances. For instance, you might temporarily modify your boundaries to help a family member who is experiencing a crisis and needs your support. It's crucial to ensure that these modifications are only brief exceptions rather than long-term ones and convey them effectively.

Feeling less guilty can also be achieved by considering the advantages of setting and maintaining boundaries. Consider the effects of upholding your boundaries on your relationships, general quality of life, and mental and emotional well-being. Take note of the better relationships with people, less stress, and more sense of control. These beneficial adjustments can reaffirm the significance of limits and give you greater self-assurance while enforcing them.

In conclusion, enforcing boundaries is vital for maintaining mental and emotional well-being, fostering self-respect, and ensuring healthy relationships. Establishing and upholding boundaries is a crucial part of self-care, even when guilt can make it more difficult to enforce them. Effective boundary enforcement involves anticipating opposition, being consistent, communicating clearly and assertively, and asking for help when needed. You can reinforce your commitment to upholding limits by controlling and rephrasing guilt, exercising flexibility when required, and considering the advantages of setting and enforcing boundaries. You can live a more balanced and satisfying life and ensure your needs are met by setting and upholding boundaries guilt-free.

CHAPTER V

Conflict Resolution

Understanding Conflict Dynamics

In both personal and professional contexts, managing and resolving conflicts successfully requires understanding conflict dynamics. Diverse factors can give rise to conflict, which takes on myriad forms and need specific approaches for its resolution. People can improve their ability to handle conflicts, cultivate stronger bonds with one another, and create a more peaceful atmosphere by investigating the different forms and origins of conflict. This section explores the many forms of conflict and the reasons behind them, offering a thorough grasp of conflict dynamics.

There are other categories into which conflict can be generally divided, such as intrapersonal, interpersonal, intergroup, and organizational conflicts. Individuals can experience interpersonal conflict frequently caused by differences in personalities, interests, values, or views. This kind of conflict can occur in professional settings between coworkers or superiors and subordinates and in personal relationships such as those between friends, family, or love partners. Interpersonal conflicts can be resolved through excellent communication and negotiation techniques, from little disagreements to major disputes.

Conversely, intrapersonal conflict occurs within a person and entails internal conflicts or struggles. Conflicts of this kind frequently occur when someone has conflicting needs, wants, or objectives. For instance, an intrapersonal conflict could arise if a person has to decide between pursuing a riskier hobby and a steady career. Understanding one's priorities, reflecting on oneself, and making choices that are consistent with one's long-term objectives and personal values are all necessary for resolving intrapersonal conflict.

Within an organization or community, intergroup conflict arises when various groups or teams interact with one another. These disputes are frequently caused by rivalry for resources, divergent aims and purposes, or conflicts between cultures and ideologies. Because intergroup disputes involve numerous parties with vested interests, they can be challenging to manage. Cooperation, mediation, and a focus on shared objectives are necessary for the effective resolution of intergroup conflicts to heal divisions and promote cooperation.

Disagreements that emerge in a structured environment—like a workplace, institution, or corporation—are categorized as organizational conflict. Hierarchical systems, ambiguous roles and responsibilities, poor communication, or different management philosophies can all contribute to these disputes. Disagreements inside a company can have far-reaching effects on morale, production, and overall effectiveness. Organizational restructuring, changes to policies, and the use of conflict resolution techniques are frequently necessary in order to resolve these disputes.

There are many different types of conflict, however they can be broadly classified into a few main areas, such as power dynamics, communication problems, resource allocation, conflicting values, and personality conflicts. Conflicts frequently arise from the distribution of resources, especially in settings with limited supplies of goods, money, or time. As people or organizations fight for a fair share of these resources, competition can cause arguments and stress. Fair allocation and efficient resource management are essential to reduce conflict in this domain.

Another major cause of conflict is poor communication. Disagreements can arise from misunderstandings, unclear communication, and poor communication channels. Conflict can arise from misunderstandings and presumptions that arise from poor communication between individuals or groups. Reducing disputes resulting from communication problems can be achieved by strengthening communication skills, maintaining transparency, and creating an atmosphere where candid discussion is valued.

Conflict often arises from differences in values and views. These disparities might stem from ideological, religious, or cultural roots and give rise to deep-seated disputes about what is proper or appropriate. Conflicts may emerge in a multicultural company where employees have differing expectations about work practices, holidays, and dress requirements. Finding common ground or making concessions that respect differing viewpoints are necessary for handling these disputes, as well as sensitivity and respect for diversity.

Conflict often arises from personality conflicts as well. It might be difficult for people with different temperaments, work methods, or interpersonal philosophies to collaborate well. An extremely meticulous person, for instance, might not get along with someone who is more adaptable and impulsive. Conflicts resulting from personality variations can be lessened by acknowledging and respecting the diversity of personality types and by creating an atmosphere of understanding and tolerance.

Hierarchical systems and power relationships can also be major causes of conflict. When power is not allocated fairly, people who have less authority may feel oppressed or marginalized, which can breed animosity and conflict. On the other hand, people in positions of power could find it difficult to exercise effective delegation or maintain control, which could cause conflict with subordinates. Creating inclusive settings, advancing equity, and ensuring that all views are heard and respected are all part of addressing power dynamics.

External pressures and developments, such as market demands, technical advancements, or economic downturns, can also give birth to conflict. These outside influences have the potential to cause tension and uncertainty, which can spark arguments when people and organizations find it challenging to adjust. Support networks, transparent communication regarding changes, and proactive change management can all lessen the adverse effects of outside influences on conflict dynamics.

Recognizing that disputes are a normal aspect of human contact and that they can have both positive and bad consequences is essential to understanding conflict dynamics. Effectively handled disagreements can foster growth, creativity, and stronger relationships, whereas unresolved conflicts can cause stress, lost productivity, and damaged relationships. The secret to maximizing conflict's good potential is to approach it proactively and constructively.

A complex strategy including open communication, active listening, empathy, and problem-solving abilities, is needed for effective conflict resolution. Establishing a space where disagreements can be handled honestly and without fear of reprisal is crucial. While conflict resolution training can equip people to handle disagreements more skillfully, mediation and negotiating approaches can assist parties in coming to mutually beneficial solutions.

In conclusion, understanding conflict dynamics involves recognizing the different types and sources of conflict that can arise in various contexts. Every type of conflict—intrapersonal, interpersonal, intergroup, and organizational—has different features and needs a different strategy to be resolved. Power dynamics, disagreements over values, communication problems, resource distribution, and personality conflicts are common causes of conflict. Individuals and organizations can effectively manage conflicts by proactively and constructively addressing these sources, so transforming potential disputes into opportunities for growth, collaboration, and improved relationships. Conflicts can be managed in ways that advance harmony and understanding between parties by developing conflict resolution skills and creating open, welcoming environments.

Resolution Techniques

Constructive conflict resolution is an essential skill for both personal and professional contexts. Addressing disagreements that foster mutual respect, collaboration, and long-term solutions is critical to effective conflict resolution. People can resolve disagreements by using systematic approaches, which reduce negative effects and promote positive results. This section examines several approaches to constructive conflict resolution, emphasizing the value of dialogue, empathy, problem-solving, and negotiation.

Establishing a respectful and tranquil atmosphere is the first step towards constructive conflict resolution. Strong feelings have the potential to intensify disputes, making constructive communication challenging. It is critical to approach the matter with a cooperative mindset and an openness to comprehending the other party's viewpoint. Providing a neutral environment where everyone feels free to voice their opinions without worrying about consequences is essential. This could entail deciding on a private area, establishing guidelines for civil dialogue, and ensuring everyone is dedicated to reaching an agreement.

A key element of constructive conflict resolution is active listening. This entails paying close attention to what they are saying, expressing empathy, and acknowledging their emotions. Building trust and demonstrating to the other person that their problems are being taken seriously are two benefits of active listening. Enhancing comprehension and avoiding misunderstandings can be achieved by using strategies including nodding, keeping eye contact, and summarizing the speaker's words. A simple statement like "I understand that you're frustrated because you feel your contributions are not being recognized" might help to both validate the speaker's feelings and start a conversation.

Determining the root causes of the conflict is crucial when a polite atmosphere and active listening techniques have been implemented. Conflicts frequently result from deeper, unmet wants or worries. Parties can strive toward more effective solutions by concentrating on the underlying causes rather than the symptoms at the surface. To investigate the underlying problems, this calls for open-ended inquiries like, "What specific actions or behaviors are causing you to feel this way?" and "Can you explain what you need to feel more supported in this situation?" Finding the underlying reasons of a conflict enables a more thorough understanding of it and makes it easier to find solutions that deal with its main problems.

Effective conflict resolution also entails assertively and clearly stating one's own wants and concerns. In order to communicate wants and feelings without coming across as judgmental, it's critical to employ "I" phrases. For instance, rather than stating, "You never listen to me," one could add, "I feel unheard when my suggestions are overlooked during meetings." This method lessens defensiveness and promotes an honest and fruitful conversation. It is easier to avoid misconceptions and make sure everyone is aware of the problems at hand when one is explicit and clear about one's wants.

Constructive conflict resolution relies heavily on the use of collaborative problem-solving techniques. This entails cooperating to provide solutions that meet the requirements of every party. Considering various possibilities and weighing their advantages and disadvantages might produce innovative solutions that benefit both parties. It's critical to maintain your flexibility and open-mindedness during this process, considering different viewpoints and options. If two coworkers are at odds about project duties, for instance, they could devise creative ways to divide the work or work together more successfully so that everyone feels appreciated and supported.

Another crucial stage in resolving disputes amicably is negotiation. This entails identifying points of agreement and consensus that satisfy everyone. To negotiate effectively, one must be prepared to make concessions and realize that the ultimate objective is to reach a win-win agreement. Negotiation success can be facilitated by employing strategies including compromising, setting priorities for essential topics, and looking into alternate options. In the event of a dispute over resource allocation at work, for example, the parties involved may agree to a fair distribution of resources that, while not perfect, satisfies everyone's demands to some degree.

Emotional control and composure are critical throughout the conflict resolution process. Feelings like rage, irritation, and resentment can impair judgment and make communicating difficult. Deep breathing, taking pauses, and engaging in mindfulness exercises are among techniques that might support emotional control and a composed appearance. People who maintain their composure are better able to think clearly, communicate effectively, and approach a problem with clarity and focus.

A crucial but frequently disregarded phase in conflict resolution is follow-up. It's critical to keep an eye on the situation and make sure the resolution is operating as planned after coming to a decision or putting a solution into action. To reinforce the settlement and avert more disputes, it is helpful to follow up with all parties concerned to find out how they are feeling and to handle any unresolved matters. For instance, a manager may arrange frequent check-ins once a disagreement over team responsibilities has been resolved to ensure that everything is going as planned and that any new issues are quickly resolved.

In conclusion, resolving conflicts constructively involves a series of deliberate steps aimed at promoting understanding, cooperation, and sustainable solutions.

Effective conflict resolution requires creating a polite and calm atmosphere, actively listening, seeing underlying problems, clearly communicating demands, working together to solve problems, negotiating, controlling emotions, and following up. By using these strategies, people can resolve disagreements in a way that minimizes their bad effects and maximizes their good ones, which promotes happier relationships and more fruitful interactions. In addition to settling conflicts, constructive conflict resolution aims to forge closer bonds and foster an atmosphere where all parties are valued, heard, and respected.

When to Walk Away

Knowing when to leave a disagreement is one of the most essential skills that can save time, energy, and emotional health. Certain disagreements cannot be settled, even though many can be through dialogue, compromise, and negotiation. Maintaining a healthy environment and safeguarding one's mental health require knowing when to back down from a conflict. This section explores the signs of unsolvable conflicts, the reasons for walking away, and the benefits of recognizing when it is time to let go.

Unresolvable conflicts frequently have particular traits that prevent them from being resolved. The main indicator is a basic mismatch in values or objectives. Finding common ground can be quite challenging when the persons involved have firmly held opinions or radically different goals. For example, in the workplace, a conflict may be unsolvable because of an intrinsic mismatch of ideals if one individual favors secrecy and manipulation while another loves transparency and honesty.

Refusing concessions is another sign that a dispute cannot be resolved. To reach a mutually beneficial conclusion, both parties must make concessions. The issue will likely not be resolved if one or both parties are adamant in their position and will not entertain different viewpoints or concessions. This rigidity frequently results from ingrained problems like ego, fear, or unresolved grudges that obscure the chance of reaching a compromise.

It might also be time to leave if there are persistent patterns of conduct that fuel the tension. When the same problems keep coming up in spite of efforts to fix them, it means that the underlying issue is not getting fixed. This may result in a vicious cycle of dissatisfaction and animosity, which intensifies the dispute. In interpersonal relationships, this could show up as constant disagreements about the same subjects, while in work environments, it might take the form of continuous conflicts about duties or work procedures.

Abuse and toxicity are important considerations when deciding when to end a confrontation. Prioritizing one's own safety and well-being is crucial when there is verbal, emotional, or physical abuse occurring throughout the conflict. Remaining in an abusive relationship in the hopes of finding a solution can have detrimental effects on one's physical and mental health. It is essential for self-preservation to recognize the warning signals of abuse and to comprehend that some issues cannot be resolved in a poisonous environment.

Another crucial factor to consider is how the disagreement may affect one's emotional and mental well-being. Extended periods of time spent in unresolved dispute can cause fatigue, stress, anxiety, and depression. It could be essential to take a step back and consider whether it's still worth it to continue the conflict when the emotional toll gets too high. Relocating can offer the necessary room for recovery and the restoration of equilibrium and overall health.

Resolving a quarrel does not imply giving up or giving in to defeat. Rather, it is a calculated choice to safeguard oneself and prioritize what really counts. Acknowledging that certain disagreements cannot be resolved helps relieve people of the stress of attempting to correct an unresolvable circumstance. They can concentrate their energies on more fruitful and satisfying activities because to this clarity.

The chance for personal growth and development is one of the main advantages of ending an unwinnable argument. Releasing yourself from a harmful or counterproductive circumstance might create fresh opportunities and paths toward improvement. It enables people to refocus their time and efforts on relationships and objectives that support their values and enhance their general well-being. Increased happiness, contentment, and satisfaction may result from this change of perspective.

Resolving an unresolvable issue can improve career development and job satisfaction in professional contexts. Remaining in a workplace where there is a lot of conflict and strain can limit prospects and impede professional development. People who know when to step away from a situation might look for new positions or groups that fit their values, abilities, and professional goals. This proactive strategy can create a more encouraging and upbeat work atmosphere that promotes both personal and professional success.

By establishing appropriate limits, stepping away from a disagreement can also strengthen bonds between people. Knowing when a disagreement cannot be resolved in a personal connection enables people to set firm boundaries for the kinds of actions they will accept. Establishing boundaries is crucial to preserving mutual understanding and respect in partnerships. Additionally, it conveys the idea that one values themselves and will not put up with rude or damaging behavior.

Furthermore, resolving problems amicably might increase one's sense of empowerment and self-efficacy. It takes courage and bravery to decide to walk away from a disagreement. It entails being aware of one's own needs and acting proactively to safeguard them. This empowerment can have a knock-on effect, enhancing the value of assertiveness and self-care and positively impacting other aspects of life.

Nonetheless, choosing to end a disagreement should not be made hastily. When making this choice, it is crucial to carefully evaluate the circumstances and consider every possible course of action. Seeking advice from dependable friends, mentors, or experts can offer insightful viewpoints and assistance during this process. It's also critical to make sure the other person knows why you've decided to go by explaining your decision politely and straightforwardly.

In conclusion, recognizing when to walk away from an unsolvable conflict is a crucial skill that can protect one's mental and emotional health, foster personal growth, and improve overall well-being. Fundamental incompatibility of values, a resistance to compromise, recurrent behavioral patterns, toxicity, and a major emotional impact are all indicators that a conflict is insoluble. Redirecting energy toward more positive and gratifying endeavors, setting appropriate boundaries, and fostering a sense of empowerment are all made possible by walking away from such situations. While disengaging is a strategic move to prioritize one's own well-being and create a more harmonious and balanced life, it should be made cautiously and wisely.

CHAPTER VI

Dealing with Different Types of Difficult People

The Narcissist

Because narcissistic people are so self-centered and lack empathy, dealing with them can be quite difficult. A need for adoration, a sense of entitlement, and grandiosity are characteristics that narcissists frequently display. Because of their propensity to put their needs and wants ahead of others, these traits can make relationships with them especially challenging. This section examines methods for handling narcissistic people in relationships in an efficient manner, emphasizing the need to preserve one's own well-being throughout these problematic situations.

Setting strong, unambiguous boundaries is one of the first things to do when dealing with a narcissist. To obtain what they want, narcissists frequently show little regard for the boundaries of others and may try to manipulate or exploit them. Establishing and upholding limits will help you keep yourself from being exploited. For example, you must politely convey your boundaries if a narcissistic coworker keeps trying to shove work onto you. You might say, "I can help you with this project for an hour, but I need to focus on my own tasks afterward." Consistency is key; repeatedly reinforcing your boundaries helps to ensure that they are respected.

Realistically managing your expectations is another key tactic. Because narcissists frequently lack the self-awareness required for personal growth, it is doubtful that they will significantly alter their behavior. You can avoid dissatisfaction and modify your expectations by realizing this. Consider what you can control: your answers and reactions, rather than wishing for empathy or understanding from others. By acknowledging the narcissist's limits, you can engage with them in a more calculated manner and lessen the emotional damage caused by unfulfilled expectations.

When interacting with narcissists, it's also critical to keep your distance emotionally. These people have a strong manipulative streak; they may sway others with charm, flattery, or even threats. You may lessen their influence on your wellbeing by controlling your emotions and avoiding taking their actions personally. Maintaining a certain amount of objectivity is what is meant by practicing detachment, not being apathetic. For instance, attempt to see unfavorable criticism from a narcissistic family member as a reflection of their fears rather than a reliable estimation of your value.

Good communication is essential while with narcissists. This calls for communicating in a clear, succinct, and assertive manner. To avoid misconceptions, it can be helpful to be clear because narcissists frequently manipulate people and circumstances. To communicate your wants and sentiments without coming across as accusing, use "I" sentences. For example, "I feel disrespected when my ideas are dismissed without consideration." By using this strategy, defensiveness can be reduced and more fruitful dialogue can ensue. Furthermore, by choosing assertiveness over passivity or aggression, you may make sure your opinion is heard without worsening the situation.

Reducing the narcissist's opportunities for manipulation is also beneficial. Narcissists love to be in charge, and they frequently use obligation, fear, or guilt to control other people. Understanding these strategies will help you better defend against manipulation. When a narcissistic buddy tries to guilt-trip you into doing something you don't want to do, for example, answer with a composed, strong "I understand your perspective, but I cannot do that." You can counteract their deceptive tactics and reaffirm your limits by maintaining your ground.

Another successful tactic is to ask for assistance from others. It can be exhausting to deal with a narcissist, but having a support system can offer consolation and valuable guidance. A therapist, family member, or friend can provide viewpoints that affirm your experiences and assist you in creating coping mechanisms. Talking about your experiences with others you can trust might also make you feel less alone and more capable of overcoming the obstacles the narcissist throws at you.

Taking care of oneself is crucial while handling relationships with narcissistic people. Your physical and emotional well-being may suffer due to the emotional strain these relationships cause. Give priority to pursuits that enhance well-being, such as physical activity, hobbies, and relaxation methods. Taking care of yourself regularly might help you stay resilient and lessen the damaging effects of the narcissist's actions. For instance, practicing mindfulness meditation can assist you in maintaining your composure and attention, making managing difficult situations simpler.

It might be essential in some circumstances to curtail or terminate your relationship with the narcissist. It could be preferable to keep your distance from them if their behavior is destructive regularly and you have tried in vain to set limits and communicate effectively. Making this choice might be especially challenging if the narcissist is a member of your family or someone you hold in high regard. But sometimes, putting your health first means having to make difficult decisions. If breaking up is not an option, think about minimizing the time you spend with them to reduce your exposure to their poisonous behavior.

Gaining a more profound comprehension of narcissistic conduct may also prove advantageous. Learning more about narcissism can help you deal with the person more skillfully and give you an understanding of why they act the way they do. Books, articles, and counseling can provide a wealth of knowledge and strategies for handling these difficult relationships. You can handle situations with more empathy and less annoyance if you realize that narcissism frequently stems from ingrained fears and a need for approval.

Dealing with a narcissistic coworker or supervisor can be especially difficult in work environments. It's critical to record conversations and keep accurate records of any instances of abuse or manipulation. This paperwork may be essential if you need to report the problem to human resources or senior management. Furthermore, concentrating on your own achievements and accomplishments can help you keep up a good reputation and defend yourself against the narcissist's attempts to discredit you.

In conclusion, managing narcissistic people necessitates a blend of distinct boundaries, reasonable expectations, emotional detachment, proficient communication, and self-nurturing. Being aware of the telltale indications of narcissism and comprehending the dynamics at work will make it easier for you to handle these difficult relationships. You may lessen the harmful effects of narcissistic behavior and continue to engage in better relationships by putting your well-being first and getting help when you need it. Although managing a narcissist is rarely simple, you can safeguard yourself and the relationship more positively by using these techniques.

The Passive-Aggressive Person

Instead of confronting problems head-on, people who engage in passive-aggressive conduct use indirect means to communicate their discontent, resentment, or wrath. This is a type of hidden negativity. Maintaining positive relationships and productive communication requires an understanding of and response to passive-aggressive behavior. This section investigates the traits of passive-aggressive people, the underlying reasons for their actions, and practical methods for controlling and lessening the effects of passive-aggression.

Because passive-aggressive conduct frequently takes subtle, indirect forms, it can be difficult to recognize. Typical indicators include procrastination, sarcasm, backhanded compliments, deliberate inefficiency, and silent treatment. These actions are intended to convey resistance or discontent without engaging in physical conflict. For instance, a coworker who exhibits passive-aggressive behavior may promise to finish a task but repeatedly put it off, creating annoyance and disruption without outright refusing to execute the work. The first step in treating passive-aggressive conduct is identifying these patterns.

The root causes of violent and passive-aggressive conduct are complex and differ from person to person. Passive-aggressive people frequently find it difficult to express their feelings openly because they are afraid of being confronted, have low self-esteem, or have learnt behaviors from their childhood. Passive-aggressive behavior might occasionally be a coping technique cultivated in settings that prohibited or penalized upfront emotional expression. Understanding these underlying causes will help you better understand why someone can act in a passive-aggressive manner and how to deal with it.

Establishing boundaries, communicating clearly, and demonstrating empathy are all necessary when dealing with passive-aggressive conduct. Comprehending the emotions and reasons underlying the passive-aggressive conduct is a crucial aspect of empathy. By demonstrating empathy, you can make the person feel more comfortable expressing their actual emotions. For instance, if a friend frequently employs sarcasm to express their anger, you could respond with something like, "I sense that you're upset about something." Could we discuss what's on your mind? In addition to promoting open communication, this strategy gives the passive-aggressive individual a sense of being heard and understood.

Effective and assertive communication is crucial when interacting with those who exhibit passive-aggressive behavior. It's critical to face the conduct head-on without getting hostile. Express how their actions impact you using "I" sentences, then ask them to give their side of the story. Say, "I noticed that you've been giving me the silent treatment after our last conversation," as an example. I'm worried and want to know what's happening. By using this approach, defensiveness is reduced and a productive conversation can begin.

Establishing and implementing limits is an essential tactic in handling passive-aggressive conduct. Passive-aggressive people frequently push boundaries to see how far they can get away with. This is something you can stop by establishing boundaries and consequences that are explicit. For instance, you could set deadlines and explain the repercussions of missing them if a coworker consistently puts off completing assignments. This methodology upholds the significance of accountability while diminishing the potential for passive-aggressive conduct to cause disturbances in the workflow.

When dealing with passive-aggressive conduct, consistency is crucial. Passive-aggressive people will try to gauge your commitment to upholding the boundaries by repeating their actions, so responding and enforcing them consistently is critical. You can make it extremely evident that passive-aggressive conduct is unacceptable and will be dealt with whenever it arises by continuously addressing the behavior and enforcing boundaries.

Encouragement of direct and honest communication is another successful strategy. Establish a space where people feel comfortable expressing their true feelings and thoughts. Regular check-ins, open-door policy, and active listening techniques might all be part of this. Individuals who perceive that their opinions are acknowledged and appreciated are less inclined to utilize passive-aggressive conduct as a mode of communication. For instance, in a team environment, you may schedule frequent meetings where team members may share their problems and provide constructive criticism in a safe environment.

Giving constructive criticism to people who behave in a passive-aggressive manner is also crucial. Give solutions or alternatives while concentrating on particular behaviors rather than making generalizations. For example, you might say, "I've noticed that you often make sarcastic comments during meetings," instead of "You're always passive-aggressive." To help us address your issues, I would appreciate it if you could be more explicit in how you voiced them. This method provides a clear path for change while assisting the person in understanding the effects of their conduct.

In certain situations, getting expert assistance might be required. In cases where passive-aggressive behavior is creating substantial disruption or is firmly rooted, therapy or counseling can be beneficial sources of support. A mental health specialist can assist the person in investigating the root causes of their behavior and creating more effective communication techniques. For instance, cognitive-behavioral therapy, or CBT, has been shown to be useful in assisting people in identifying and altering harmful thought and behavior patterns.

Taking care of your personal health is also crucial while interacting with passive-aggressive people. Handling passive-aggressive behavior can be emotionally taxing, therefore self-care must come first. This could entail scheduling downtime for unwinding, asking friends and family for help, and engaging in stress-relieving activities like exercise or mindfulness. Maintaining your personal health will enable you to deal with the difficulties that passive-aggressive behavior presents.

In the end, dealing with passive-aggressive conduct calls for endurance, perseverance, and a dedication to promoting constructive dialogue. Dealing with subliminal negativity can be annoying, but it can also result in great improvements if you handle the situation with clarity, empathy, and consistency. By promoting candid communication, establishing unambiguous boundaries, and offering helpful criticism, you can foster an atmosphere that is less conducive to passive-aggressive conduct.

In conclusion, identifying and dealing with passive-aggressive conduct necessitates knowledge of its traits, underlying reasons, and practical management techniques. Setting boundaries, communicating clearly, showing empathy, and maintaining consistency are all essential when with passive-aggressive people. Positive improvements can also be supported by promoting honest and open conversation, offering helpful criticism, and, when required, obtaining expert assistance. You may overcome the difficulties posed by passive-aggressive behavior and encourage healthier, more positive connections by caring for your wellbeing and creating a supportive environment.

The Chronic Complainer

Handling chronic complainers can be a big problem in both personal and professional contexts. These people frequently communicate their pessimism and unhappiness incessantly, which can deplete the vitality and spirits of people around them. Nonetheless, understanding, sensitivity, and tactful communication can turn persistent hostility into productive conversation. This section explores the characteristics of chronic complainers, the underlying reasons for their behavior, and effective strategies to engage them in more positive and productive conversations.

People who routinely voice their displeasure and concentrate on issues rather than solutions are known as chronic complainers. No matter how small the problem may be, they frequently draw attention to what is incorrect in any given circumstance. This conduct can take many forms, such as constant complaining, exaggerated displays of annoyance, and a generally gloomy attitude. Those who frequently engage with the complainer may find their mood and productivity negatively impacted by the persistent negativity, which can also create a toxic environment. Constructively resolving persistent complaint begins with identifying the patterns and motivations underlying this behavior.

Converting negative discussions requires an understanding of the root causes of persistent complaining. Chronic complainers frequently have a need for approval and attention. Their grievances could be an outlet for repressed emotions of inadequacy, dissatisfaction, or powerlessness. Some people learn to complain from their parents or from earlier situations where their bad behavior won them sympathy or attention. Furthermore, people who complain a lot might not have good coping strategies for handling stress, which makes them feel frustrated and inclined to complain all the time. Understanding these elements can help you better adjust your tactics to deal with their conduct.

Managing persistent complainers requires a great deal of empathy. Demonstrating real care and empathy can establish a supportive environment where the complainant feels heard. Recognizing the experiences and sentiments of the complainant is a sign of empathy rather than endorsing the complaints. Say, "I see that you're really frustrated with this situation," as an example. It seems that things haven't been easy for you. This method can lessen their need to behave negatively in order to get attention by validating their feelings. They might be more willing to talk about solutions if they feel heard, as opposed to merely concentrating on the issues.

Engaging in active listening is a crucial tactic when managing persistent grievers. This entails listening intently to what they say, seeking clarification when necessary, and summarizing their main ideas to ensure you understand. Establishing a rapport and demonstrating your genuine interest in the complainant's viewpoint are two benefits of active listening. For instance, you may ask, "Can you tell me more about what specifically is bothering you about this project?" in response to a coworker who is continuously grumbling about a certain project. This method assists in identifying the main problems that require attention in addition to demonstrating empathy.

One important tactic for turning complaints into productive conversation is to promote a change in perspective from one that is problem-focused to one that is solution-focused. Chronic complainers frequently find themselves in a vicious circle of negativity, only thinking about the problems rather than the possible solutions. You can assist them in developing a more positive outlook by gently directing the conversation toward solutions. You may ask, "What do you think could be done to improve this situation?" or "How can we address this issue together?" after noting their objections. This motivates the complainant to stop just expressing their frustrations and instead adopt a proactive mindset by considering concrete actions.

Establishing limits is crucial when handling persistent whiners. You must safeguard your own health and avoid becoming overwhelmed by the complainer's negativity. Negative talks can be controlled in terms of frequency and length by establishing respectful and unambiguous limits. You may say something like, "I know you're worried, but I can't talk about this right now. When I have more time later, may we discuss it? or "While I'm happy to listen, let's also concentrate on coming up with solutions." By using this strategy, you can safeguard your own mental well-being while still continuing to be supportive.

Giving persistent complainers constructive criticism might make them more conscious of their actions and how they affect other people. Feedback ought to be given in a non-confrontational way, with precision and objectivity. Saying, "I've noticed that you often express concerns about our projects during meetings," is one example of what you could say. Although it's critical to address problems, I believe it would be beneficial if we also spoke about possible solutions. This feedback draws attention to the problem and promotes a more methodical approach to tackling it.

Promoting a happy atmosphere can also lessen the impact of persistent whining. Encourage the development of a culture that values and recognizes positive contributions. This may assist in turning the conversation from negativity to optimism. For example, regular team meetings showcasing accomplishments and advancements can create a more favorable work environment. Creating an atmosphere that rewards good behavior can help those who are always complaining feel less motivated to dwell on the bad things.

It could be essential in some circumstances to work with a mediator or get expert assistance. A mediator or counselor, for example, is an impartial third party who can assist in facilitating more productive conversation if persistent complaint is seriously disrupting the group dynamic and negatively impacting morale. They can offer methods for resolving fundamental problems and enhancing the dynamic as a whole. Professional assistance may be especially helpful if the complainant's behavior is strongly rooted or connected to unresolved personal difficulties.

In conclusion, dealing with chronic complainers involves the use of empathy, active listening, and strategic communication to turn their persistent negativity into productive discourse. In this process, it's critical to comprehend the underlying causes of their conduct, express genuine concern, and promote solution-focused thinking. Setting limits, giving helpful criticism, and encouraging a pleasant atmosphere can all help these initiatives. Although managing persistent complainers might be difficult, these techniques can assist in transforming unfavorable discussions into chances for development and enhancement, ultimately promoting happier and more fruitful relationships. Using these strategies may foster a more encouraging and friendly atmosphere where fruitful discussion flourishes.

The Bully

Managing bullies necessitates striking a delicate balance between firmness and poise in order to confront aggressive conduct without making things worse. Bullies can seriously injure others emotionally and psychologically. They control and dominate others via intimidation and hostility. This section discusses methods for identifying bullying behavior, dealing with it constructively, and confronting bullies without making things worse. It emphasizes the value of assertive communication, establishing boundaries, and asking for help.

The first step in dealing with bullying behavior is recognizing it. Bullies frequently employ a variety of strategies, such as physical intimidation, verbal abuse, and social manipulation, to establish their authority. They might make threats to arouse fear, propagate rumors, or denigrate or humiliate their targets. It is essential to comprehend these actions to recognize bullying and take necessary response. A coworker who consistently disparages your work, disseminates untrue information about you, or speaks angrily is engaging in bullying behavior. Being aware of these tendencies enables you to react more forcefully and successfully.

Assertive communication is one of the most essential strategies for confronting bullies without making things worse. Directly and respectfully expressing your needs, wants, and views is a sign of assertiveness. It entails responding to the bullying conduct in a cool, collected manner. For instance, you could respond, "I don't like being spoken to in that way," if a bully is using disparaging language. Please show me some consideration." This strategy effectively communicates your point without using hostility or inaction. Two benefits of assertive communication are setting limits and making it clear that disrespectful behavior won't be tolerated.

Another crucial tactic for dealing with bullies is to set boundaries. Boundaries serve to safeguard your mental and emotional health by defining appropriate behavior. Setting and maintaining these limits is essential when interacting with a bully. For instance, if a coworker regularly interrupts you or invades your personal space, you can firmly and calmly say, "I need you to respect my personal space and allow me to finish speaking." You may convey your expectations and lessen the bully's possibilities to act aggressively by establishing clear boundaries. Maintaining consistency is essential; you can ensure your boundaries are respected by constantly reiterating them.

Keeping your emotional reactions under control is crucial when interacting with bullies. Bullies frequently feed off their victims' emotional responses, utilizing them as a means of reiterating their control. Remaining calm and not displaying any symptoms of anger or fear can aid in disarming the bully. Practices like mindfulness, deep breathing, and grounding exercises can assist you in maintaining composure and concentration in stressful situations. For example, breathing deeply a few times before answering a bully who is verbally abusing you can help you stay calm and respond assertively instead of reactively.

One of the most important aspects of dealing with bullying is asking for help from others. Isolating their targets is a common tactic used by bullies to keep control. By establishing connections with friends, family, coworkers, or superiors, you can create a network of support that offers both practical help and emotional validation. Speaking with reliable people about the bullying behavior will help you come up with fresh ideas and solutions for handling the problem. In the workplace, bringing up the matter with a manager or human resources representative can assist to formalize the conversation and guarantee that the necessary actions are taken. Having other people's support can help you become more resilient and confident, which will make it simpler to confront the bully.

Another crucial instrument for combating bullying is documentation, particularly in settings that are professional. If you need to escalate the matter, having a thorough record of bullying incidents—including dates, timings, descriptions of the behavior, and names of any witnesses—can be useful information. Formal complaints or legal actions may require a clear and impartial account of the bullying, which can be produced with the aid of documentation. For instance, recording the times a bully continuously makes disparaging remarks during meetings may help you make a stronger case to management or HR when you report the behavior.

It's critical to confront bullying by concentrating on the conduct rather than the victim. This strategy promotes positive communication and de-escalates the situation. For example, you could say, "I find your comments and actions towards me disrespectful and hurtful," as opposed to, "You are a bully." This avoids identifying the person, which can cause defensiveness and more conflict, and concentrates on the precise behaviors that need to be altered. Resolution and transformation may be facilitated by immediately and constructively addressing the problem.

In certain situations, it could be advisable to leave the bully alone to prevent the situation from worsening. De-escalating the situation can be helpful if the bully is not amenable to aggressive conversation or if the situation gets too hot. Walking away is a calculated action to safeguard your safety and stop the situation from worsening. It does not imply giving up to the bully. For instance, saying, "I am going to step away now and continue this discussion later" can help diffuse a situation when a bully starts acting more aggressively during a talk.

If bullying doesn't go away even after you try to handle it, you might need to report the matter to higher authorities. This could entail bringing up the issue in writing with the human resources department of your company, getting legal counsel, or getting in touch with pertinent outside organizations like labor boards or trade associations. If you want to improve your case, you should escalate the matter with the assistance of any supporting paperwork and witnesses. To effectively address bullying and safeguard your rights, make sure you adhere to the proper channels and processes.

Bullying prevention and intervention can also be significantly aided by education and training. Employers ought to train staff members to spot and deal with bullying while fostering an inclusive and respectful workplace culture. With this knowledge, people will be more equipped to confront bullying head-on and foster a welcoming climate where bullying is less likely to flourish. Workshops on emotional intelligence, assertive communication, and conflict resolution, for instance, can give staff members the tools they need to deal with bullying productively.

In conclusion, standing up to bullying requires a combination of assertive communication, boundary-setting, emotional regulation, and support-seeking. De-escalating the situation and asserting your rights can be facilitated by identifying bullying behavior and confronting it with dignity and directness. Dealing with bullies requires maintaining composure, asking for help, recording events, and concentrating on the behavior rather than the individual. Formal procedures like reporting the matter to higher authorities can be required if bullying doesn't stop. Using these techniques, people can safeguard their well-being, promote a respectful environment, and deal with violent conduct in a productive way without making things worse.

The Victim

Assisting people who believe they are victims for life can be a challenging but worthwhile undertaking. These people frequently experience a sense of helplessness because they think outside factors dictate their situations and that they have little to no control over their lives. A vicious circle of hopelessness, pessimism, and self-fulfilling prophecies can result from this victim attitude. It's critical to provide empathy, support, and techniques that enable those who perceive themselves as lifelong victims to take charge of their circumstances and cultivate a more optimistic and proactive outlook. This section examines the traits of a victim mentality, their underlying causes, and practical solutions for assisting these people in changing their viewpoint and regaining their agency.

Victim mentality is characterized by several traits, such as an unwillingness to accept responsibility for one's actions, a propensity to attribute problems to outside forces, and a chronic feeling of helplessness. They frequently have a pessimistic outlook on life, feeling they have little control over their circumstances and that horrible things will inevitably happen. This kind of thinking can show up in several ways, including persistent whining, a lack of initiative, and a reluctance to attempt new things or take chances. Helping people who perceive themselves as lifelong victims begins with identifying these patterns.

There might be many different and intricate root causes of a victim mindset. It could originate from prior traumatic, abusive, or neglectful events when the person actually had little control over their situation. These experiences have the potential to cause learned helplessness over time, in which the individual internalizes the notion that they have no power to change their surroundings. Furthermore, social and cultural elements that prioritize outside control over individual agency, like messaging, might contribute to perpetuating a victim mentality. Knowing these underlying reasons might help one better understand victim mentality and the best ways to deal with it.

To assist those who have a victim mentality, empathy is an essential quality. You may establish a secure and encouraging environment where the person feels heard and valued by genuinely empathetic and compassionate toward them. Actively listening to their worries, recognizing their emotions, and avoiding passing judgment are all parts of empathy. Saying "I can see that you're feeling really overwhelmed and it's understandable given what you've been through" is one example of what you could say. By establishing rapport and trust, this method increases the person's openness to receiving additional advice and assistance.

Another crucial tactic is to promote introspection. Enabling people to identify their own thought patterns and actions can enable them to transform their lives for the better. One way to do this could be to pose open-ended questions that encourage them to reflect on their part in the situation. One may inquire, "What do you think you could do differently to change this situation?" as an example. and "How do you think your actions are contributing to this outcome?" By encouraging a change in perspective from one of passivity to activity, these questions help the person develop a sense of agency and accountability.

Encouraging a growth attitude is essential for assisting people in overcoming a victim mentality. The idea that one's circumstances and abilities may be improved with work and education is known as a growth mindset. On the other hand, a fixed mindset—which is frequently connected to a victim mentality—sees circumstances and one's own skills as fixed and unalterable. Promoting a growth mindset entails emphasizing the importance of hard work, perseverance, and learning from failures. As an illustration, you may tell tales of people who, by tenacity and resolve, overcame great adversity. This strategy can encourage the person to see their circumstances as chances for personal development rather than insurmountable challenges.

Establishing attainable objectives is another powerful strategy for empowering those who have a victim mindset. Setting small, realistic goals might help people feel accomplished and more confident about their capacity to make a difference in their lives. Together, determine measurable, achievable goals and create a strategy to reach them. You may assist them in setting objectives to update their resume, apply for a specific number of jobs each week, or enroll in a course to improve their abilities, for instance, if they feel trapped in their employment. Honoring their accomplishments, no matter how modest, can help them feel more in control of their life and inspire them to keep moving forward.

Fighting a victim attitude also requires promoting constructive self-talk. Negative self-talk encourages powerlessness and can keep a victim cycle going. Replace negative thoughts with more empowering and uplifting ones to assist the person in identifying and combating them. Encourage them to reframe the statement, "I can't do anything right," for instance, to, "I am capable of learning and improving." They can cultivate a more productive and upbeat internal conversation with the use of teaching methods like cognitive restructuring or affirmations.

It is crucial to give people the tools and encouragement they need to shift from a victim mentality to a more empowered one. This could entail putting them in touch with support groups, counseling, therapy, and self-help books that cover topics like coping mechanisms, resilience, and self-worth. Getting professional help can be especially helpful when dealing with ingrained attitudes and behavioral patterns that are hard to break on your own. For instance, cognitive-behavioral therapy (CBT) is an empirically supported method that can assist people in recognizing and altering harmful thought patterns and behaviors.

Setting limits is crucial for assisting people who have a victim mindset. As vital as supporting and encouraging them, it is just as critical to refrain from condoning their actions. When you assume their tasks or let them evade accountability, you are enabling them. Establish limits by empowering people to accept responsibility for their choices and actions. For instance, you could say, "I'm here to support you, but it's important that you take the lead in addressing this issue," if they regularly come to you for problem-solving advice. This method supports their independence and motivates them to hone their problem-solving abilities.

In conclusion, helping individuals who see themselves as perpetual victims involves a combination of empathy, encouragement, and empowerment. You can assist them on their path to greater agency and resilience by comprehending the root causes of a victim mentality and using techniques like active listening, encouraging a growth mindset, setting realistic goals, encouraging positive self-talk, and providing the necessary resources. To ensure kids accept accountability for their choices and behaviors, it's critical to balance offering support and establishing limits. By using these strategies, people can end the cycle of victimization and cultivate a proactive, upbeat mindset that will ultimately result in a more empowered and fulfilling existence.

CHAPTER VII

Building a Support System

The Role of Support Networks

Support networks are essential for helping people deal with negative people because they offer emotional stability, helpful guidance, and a defense against the exhausting effects of persistent negativity. These networks, which usually include friends, family, and coworkers, might provide a range of viewpoints and approaches to handle and lessen the effects of unfavorable people. This section examines how these various support systems aid in dealing with negativity, highlighting the significance of empathy, communication, and group resilience.

When coping with negative people, friends are frequently the first to offer support. They provide a secure environment for expressing annoyances and exchanging personal stories without passing judgment. A friend's listening ear can be immensely beneficial, relieving tension and validating emotions. Friends can also provide helpful guidance and different perspectives that can aid in comprehending and dealing with the actions of negative people. For instance, if a friend is helping someone deal with a toxic coworker, they could offer advice on setting boundaries or provide perspective based on their personal experiences. Friends' companionship and emotional support are priceless for preserving resilience and mental health.

Family support is just as important when interacting with negative individuals. Family members can offer a secure and nurturing environment that balances out the negativity seen elsewhere, especially if they are close and supportive. Family support can come in many forms, such as practical help, emotional support, and group problem-solving. Talking to a spouse or sibling about the difficulties presented by an unfavorable employer or coworker, for example, might assist in organizing ideas and creating useful coping mechanisms. Furthermore, family members frequently have enough personal knowledge of the person to offer tailored counsel and assistance. They can support them, encourage them, and help them maintain perspective—all of which are essential for preserving mental health. They can also serve to remind them of their strengths.

Dealing with negative individuals is mostly dependent on colleagues, especially in the workplace where professional interactions and settings can have a substantial impact on mental health. Coworkers who are supportive can give helpful tips on handling challenging situations, discuss tactics that have worked for them, and foster a feeling of community. Coworkers may occasionally serve as allies in the fight against workplace negativity, offering support and reducing its adverse effects. By encouraging a healthy and inclusive work culture that discourages negative behavior, a supportive team, for instance, might collectively address the behavior of a negative coworker. Colleagues can also offer professional support, which can help to lessen the stress of dealing with negative people. Examples of this support include sharing responsibilities or offering aid on complex tasks.

Utilizing support networks is crucial for leveraging effective communication when interacting with negative people. The correct kind of assistance can be given if friends, family, and coworkers are informed about the difficulties being faced and the kind of support that is required in an open and honest manner. For example, making it obvious that you need a sympathetic ear or helpful guidance might help support networks react correctly. Furthermore, staying in constant contact with support systems helps ward against feelings of loneliness and offer continuous comfort. For instance, staying in touch with a close friend or relative on a regular basis might be a reliable source of emotional support and stability.

Support networks need to have empathy to comprehend and control the detrimental effects of negative people. Friends, relatives, and coworkers that are empathetic can validate emotions, offer consolation, and a deeper understanding of the difficulties encountered. Empathy may be a potent counterbalance to the negativity that people receive from others by fostering a supportive environment where people feel understood and respected. For example, a family member who listens to worries about an unsupportive boss might offer emotional comfort and assurance, aiding in restoring perspective and equilibrium. Additionally, empathy strengthens ties within support networks, which increases the efficacy of these networks in offering assistance.

Support networks' collective resilience can greatly improve the ability to deal with negative people. Resilience is the ability to bounce back from setbacks and keep a good attitude in the face of adversity. Through sharing experiences, providing mutual support, and bolstering constructive coping mechanisms, support networks can foster collective resilience. Friends who have dealt with negative people well, for instance, can share their tactics and experiences, offering encouragement and insightful information. Similar to this, coworkers who help one another through difficult times at work can promote a feeling of unity and group strength, which makes it simpler to resist and get past negativity.

Support networks should also promote self-care and constructive activities to cope with negative individuals.

Colleagues, friends, and family can support and engage in stress-relieving and well-being-promoting activities. Friends may recommend and partake in stress-relieving hobbies, physical activities, or social gatherings that offer a healthy way to express feelings. Family members can encourage their loved one to practice self-care by ensuring they get enough sleep, relax, and engage in enjoyable activities. Coworkers may support a good work-life balance at work by enforcing limits, allowing for breaks, and providing time off when necessary. The depleting effects of negativity can be offset by engaging in these constructive activities and self-care routines, which also assist to improve resilience in general.

Sometimes the help offered by personal support networks must be supplemented by professional support. Support groups, therapists, and counselors can provide specific advice and coping mechanisms for handling negative people. Expert assistance can give an organized setting for examining and resolving the effects of negativity and methods like cognitive-behavioral therapy (CBT) to modify unfavorable thought patterns and actions. A therapist, for example, can assist a person in strengthening resilience, coping mechanisms, and communication skills—all of which will help them better manage and lessen the negative effects of other people.

In conclusion, support systems made up of friends, family, and coworkers are essential for assisting people in coping with unfavorable people. These networks offer practical guidance, emotional support, and protection from the depleting effects of negativity. In order to manage and lessen the influence of negative people, support networks must have effective communication, empathy, and collective resilience. Promoting constructive pursuits and self-care also helps people become more adept at handling negativity. Professional assistance could be required in some circumstances to enhance personal support systems. People can use these support systems to preserve their mental health and overall well-being, proficiently handle unfavorable situations, and cultivate a more optimistic and robust perspective.

Finding Allies

Achieving both personal and professional success requires forming supportive relationships and finding allies. Allies offer people moral support, useful guidance, and a feeling of community that can aid in overcoming obstacles and achieving objectives. Finding and cultivating these relationships takes a calculated effort, emphasizing trust, respect, and similar values. This section looks at the value of having allies, how to spot helpful relationships, and how to nurture and sustain these relationships over time.

Allies are essential for both professional and personal development because they give a network of people who can offer support, advice, and encouragement. In a personal setting, allies might be mentors, friends, or family members willing to offer both practical and emotional support and aware of your goals and obstacles. Allies in the workplace might be peers, managers, or coworkers who have similar objectives and moral standards. They can also provide support, resources, and chances for cooperation. The existence of relationships that provide support can greatly improve an individual's capacity to manage stress, surmount challenges, and attain achievement.

The first step in finding possible partners is being self-aware and clear about your own needs, values, and objectives. Finding people who share your goals and values is easier when you know what kind of supportive relationship you seek. Seek out those that exhibit traits like empathy, dependability, honesty, and a sincere concern for your well. These people are more likely to care about your success and provide significant help.

Furthermore, consider the context of your encounters; allies can arise in various contexts, such as social circles, professional networks, and neighborhood associations.

One of the most important tactics for finding possible partners is networking. You can meet like-minded people by engaging in online forums, attending events, and joining organizations that are linked to your industry or interests. One can find mutual interests, have conversations, and exchange experiences through networking. For instance, going to local meetings or industry conferences can introduce you to peers facing similar career issues and objectives. Social media groups, professional forums, and online platforms like LinkedIn provide great chances to meet and establish connections with possible allies from various places and backgrounds.

Establishing trust is essential to developing connections that are beneficial. Interactions that are polite, truthful, and consistent build trust. Establishing trust is facilitated by exhibiting dependability through keeping one's word, protecting privacy, and genuinely caring about the welfare of others. For instance, when a coworker confides in you about a work-related issue, you can fortify your relationship by providing wise counsel and maintaining their confidence. Reciprocal support, in which both partners give to and gain from the relationship, is another way to strengthen trust.

Another crucial component of developing connections that are helpful is effective communication. Relationships are strengthened, disputes are resolved, and understanding is fostered by open and honest communication. Developing rapport and mutual respect can be facilitated by using essential communication skills like active listening, expressing gratitude, and giving constructive criticism. For example, asking friends or coworkers how they are doing and providing assistance shows that you appreciate and care about the relationship. In addition, maintaining an open and balanced dynamic is facilitated by being honest about your personal wants and boundaries.

In partnerships that are helpful, reciprocity is essential. Respecting the beliefs, limits, and ideas of others creates a welcoming atmosphere where people are treated with dignity and respect. This entails treating people with respect and consideration, accepting and appreciating diversity, and remaining receptive to different viewpoints. Respecting a colleague's problem-solving method, for instance, in a work environment, even if it is different from your own, might result in more creative and cooperative solutions. Recognizing and resolving any power imbalances is another aspect of mutual respect, which aims to make everyone feel valued and powerful.

A valuable skill for establishing and preserving supportive connections is empathy. Understanding and validating the thoughts, feelings, and experiences of others while providing sympathetic, nonjudgmental support are all parts of exhibiting empathy. Empathy builds trust and a sense of emotional safety amongst people. For example, lending a sympathetic ear and expressing empathy to a friend who is going through a tough moment may be incredibly reassuring and supportive. Being perceptive to nonverbal clues and being sensitive to the needs of others require empathy as well.

One key idea in building enduring connections is reciprocity. A healthy balance between providing and receiving assistance is a sign of a healthy partnership. Offering assistance, sharing resources, and encouraging others creates a mutually beneficial dynamic in which both sides feel appreciated and supported. When a coworker helps you with a project, for instance, offering to help them in return or showing your appreciation strengthens the reciprocal nature of the relationship. In order to be reciprocal, you need also be careful not to burden others with your demands and make sure that their assistance is mutually beneficial.

One important part of developing relationships that are supportive is mentoring. Mentors can aid people on their personal and professional paths by offering direction, insight, and support. Finding mentors is locating people with the expertise, understanding, and personal traits you value and respect. It takes openness to learning, a readiness to ask for and act upon feedback, and an expression of gratitude for the mentor's time and assistance to develop a relationship between mentee and mentor. The mentor-mentee relationship can be strengthened by, for instance, thanking your mentor for their thoughts and providing regular updates on your development.

In work environments, developing supportive connections requires cooperation and coordination. Working together on projects, exchanging information, and pursuing shared objectives promotes camaraderie and support among team members. Colleague trust and cooperation can be increased by organizing team-building exercises and providing cooperative problem-solving opportunities. For instance, engaging in cross-functional teams or committees can facilitate the development of relationships with coworkers from various departments, thereby establishing a network of support within the company.

In conclusion, developing supportive networks and finding allies are critical for both professional and personal development. Finding possible allies entails knowing your own objectives and principles, making connections, and spotting traits in other people like empathy, dependability, and integrity. Developing mutual respect, empathy, reciprocity, trust, and effective communication are key components of fostering these relationships. Collaborating and mentoring strengthens networks of support by offering direction and encouraging teamwork. Through deliberate identification and cultivation of supportive relationships, individuals can establish a resilient support network that facilitates their ability to overcome obstacles, accomplish their objectives, and prosper in both personal and professional domains.

Seeking Professional Help

It can be difficult and draining to deal with negative people, and it frequently calls for more assistance than friends and family can offer. In certain situations, addressing the adverse effects of negativity on one's mental and emotional health may require obtaining professional assistance. Knowing when to get professional help, what kinds of specialists are out there, and how to get these services may make a big difference in how well someone can handle and negotiate challenging relationships. The significance of seeking professional assistance, when it is proper to do so, and how to do so are all covered in this section.

Identifying when to get professional assistance is the first step in dealing with the problems that negative people bring. Even while everyone periodically comes into contact with challenging individuals, prolonged exposure to negativity can cause a great deal of stress, anxiety, and mental suffering. Overwhelmed feelings, enduring melancholy or anxiety, trouble sleeping, changes in food, and problems concentrating are signs that you might need professional help. Furthermore, it could be time to consider getting professional assistance if unfavorable interactions impair your ability to function in relationships, at work, or in general. Recognizing these indicators to take preventative measures to safeguard your mental health is essential.

Professionals of all stripes can help with handling negative individuals. The first people to help are frequently therapists and counselors. They have received training in assisting people in bettering their mental health, coping mechanism development, and emotional understanding. Counselors can assist you in examining the root causes of your tension and provide you with strategies for dealing with unfavorable people more skillfully. For instance, cognitive-behavioral therapy (CBT) can assist you in identifying and altering unfavorable thought patterns and behaviors, which will increase your emotional resilience.

Life coaches, in addition to therapists, can provide invaluable assistance. In spite of obstacles presented by unfavorable people, life coaches assist clients in identifying and achieving their goals through goal-setting and personal growth. They can offer helpful tips and methods for handling challenging relationships, improving communication abilities, and boosting self-esteem. Additionally, life coaches may assist you in building resilience and a positive outlook, which can help you deal with negativity more effectively.

Seeking assistance from human resources (HR) specialists or employee assistance programs (EAPs) might be helpful for workplace-related concerns. Human resources specialists possess the necessary skills to manage workplace conflicts, harassment, and other challenges that may emerge from dealing with unfavorable coworkers or managers. They can act as conflict mediators, put regulations in place to guarantee a polite workplace, and offer resources for additional assistance. To assist staff in overcoming obstacles at work, EAPs frequently include workshops, stress management courses, and private counseling services.

There are various processes involved in locating the best expert support. Determine your unique wants and concerns first. Think about whether you require assistance with work-related concerns, practical relationship management techniques, or emotional support. This clarity will help you select the right specialist. The next step is to look into potential coaches, counselors, or therapists. Seek experts who focus on managing stress, anxiety, relationships with others, or workplace dynamics. Making an educated choice can be aided by reading reviews, getting recommendations, and confirming credentials.

After you've found several possible experts, set up first sessions to talk through your issues and see whether they're a suitable fit. Numerous coaches and therapists provide free initial sessions, allowing you to assess their style and determine whether you're comfortable working with them. Ask them about their methods, experience, and how they may help you with your particular difficulties during these appointments. Establishing a rapport and experiencing understanding are critical components of a fruitful therapeutic or coaching alliance.

Expense is a significant factor to take into account when obtaining expert assistance. The cost of coaching and therapy services might vary, so it's essential to know how much you can afford and look into other payment methods. In addition to some insurance plans covering mental health care, many therapists offer sliding scale pricing based on income. Community mental health facilities may provide low-cost or subsidized services, and employee assistance programs (EAPs) frequently offer free therapy sessions for staff members. You can get the assistance you require without experiencing unnecessary stress if you know the financial side.

It's critical to approach expert assistance with an open mind and a desire to participate in the process. It takes time to adjust and work and dedication to develop new coping mechanisms and resilience. Your ability to handle relationships with negative people can be significantly improved with regular sessions and active engagement in treatment or coaching. Effective support and assistance require you to be honest with your therapist or coach about your feelings, obstacles, and progress.

Support groups can also be a great tool for overcoming negative individuals. These organizations offer a forum for exchanging experiences and picking up tips from others dealing with related issues. Support groups can lessen feelings of loneliness by providing a sense of understanding and community. Support groups are available for a variety of problems, such as anxiety, stress management, and interacting with challenging individuals, through numerous organizations and online resources. By offering other viewpoints and support, joining these groups can enhance individual treatment or coaching.

Professional assistance may occasionally need organizational or legal action. You may need to get legal counsel or involve higher authorities in your company if you are dealing with harassment, discrimination, or serious dispute at work. Addressing more serious concerns requires a clear understanding of your rights and the laws in place to protect you. HR specialists and lawyers can help you take the right actions to protect your safety and well-being.

In conclusion, seeking professional help in dealing with negative people is a vital step for protecting your mental and emotional health. Your ability to deal with negativity can be significantly improved by identifying the warning signs that you need professional help, knowing what kinds of specialists are available, and taking action to locate the correct support. Support groups, HR specialists, life coaches, and therapists are all excellent sources for handling challenging relationships and developing resilience. You can create helpful coping mechanisms for negativity and enhance your general well-being by committing to the process and keeping an open mind when seeking expert assistance.

CHAPTER VIII

Long-Term Strategies for Positive Relationships

Maintaining Positivity

Maintaining positive relationships over the long term is essential for personal well-being and overall life satisfaction. Good connections boost resilience, happiness, and a sense of belonging by offering emotional support. Mutual respect, skillful communication, and persistent effort are necessary to build and maintain these relationships. This section examines several routines and behaviors that are essential to upholding healthy relationships, highlighting the significance of common interests, communication, empathy, and trust.

Positive relationships are built on effective communication. Building trust, resolving disputes, and strengthening relationships all benefit from courteous, open, and honest communication. Mutual understanding and closeness are fostered when people share their ideas, emotions, and experiences regularly. It's essential to listen actively, which is paying close attention to what the other person is saying without interrupting or making suggestions immediately. It demonstrates your appreciation for their viewpoint and your sincere concern for their welfare. To ensure that both parties feel heard and understood, you can further improve communication by posing open-ended questions and responding to what you have heard.

Another essential element of preserving healthy connections is empathy. Understanding and experiencing another person's emotions entails empathy and fosters a strong emotional bond. Empathy is the ability to place oneself in another person's position and consider their feelings and experiences. This can be especially crucial in conflict or difficult situations. A basic way to show empathy is to acknowledge the other person's sentiments by saying something like, "I see that you're really upset about this." By acknowledging their feelings, you can let them know you are there for them and that you care.

The foundation of any healthy relationship is trust. Reliability, truthfulness, and consistency are necessary to establish and preserve trust. Building a foundation of trust involves being reliable, timely, and able to fulfill obligations. Being open and truthful is also crucial, even in the face of difficulty. When trust is lost, it can be regained by offering real regrets, taking responsibility for one's actions, and persistently working to mend the relationship. Giving others the benefit of the doubt and holding off on drawing judgments until you completely understand the circumstances at hand are other aspects of trust.

Respect for one another is necessary to keep happy relationships going. A secure and encouraging atmosphere is produced when people respect one another's limits, viewpoints, and uniqueness. It entails appreciating the viewpoint of those with whom you disagree. The link between people is strengthened when they support one another's personal development and show tolerance for one another's varying interests and preferences. In real life, this could entail respecting each other's wants and preferences, enjoying each other's successes, and offering each other space when necessary.

Maintaining healthy relationships requires regular quality time spent together. Strengthening the bond and making enduring memories can be achieved through participating in common activities and trying new things together. Simple pursuits like sharing a meal, taking a stroll, or engaging in a shared pastime might be examples of this. Making plans for frequent date nights, family vacations, or get-togethers with friends guarantees that time is set aside to strengthen the bond between them. These common experiences strengthen the ties that bind people together by fostering a sense of joy and participation.

Regularly expressing thankfulness and praise is another crucial habit. A positive environment can be created by taking the time to recognize and express gratitude to one another for both major and small things. Written notes, spoken affirmations, or tiny deeds of kindness can all help achieve this. Rewarding a friend for their loyalty and company, or expressing gratitude to a spouse for their assistance during a trying period, strengthens the relationship's positive sides. Having gratitude makes it easier to turn one's attention from unpleasant things and promotes appreciation and optimism.

Positive relationships require constructive conflict management to last a long time. Although conflicts are unavoidable, how they are managed can have a big impact. Important tactics include approaching problems coolly and politely, concentrating on the subject rather than the other person, and looking for solutions that all parties can agree on. It's critical to refrain from placing blame or bringing up old concerns because doing so can make the situation worse. Rather than assigning blame, utilize "I" phrases to communicate your wants and feelings. For example, "I feel hurt when you cancel our plans at the last minute." By promoting open communication and problem-solving, this strategy helps settle disputes without deteriorating relationships.

Sustaining positive partnerships requires that partners support one another's ambitions. Supporting and encouraging someone's professional and personal development shows that you are concerned about their success and well-being. This assistance can be given in the form of financial support, moral support, or just by acting as a sounding board for concepts and schemes. Celebrating each other's successes and milestones deepens the relationship and promotes a sense of cooperation and shared purpose.

Maintaining healthy relationships also requires forgiveness practices. Over time, harboring resentments and grudges can damage a relationship. Moving ahead requires learning to forgive and let go of the hurts from the past. To be forgiven is to let go of the bad feelings that come with cruel behavior, not to support it. For the benefit of the relationship and your own well-being, it entails admitting the hurt, expressing your emotions, and then deciding to let go. Relationships can be strengthened and healed via the practice of forgiveness, which enables mutual improvement and growth.

Another important habit is keeping a sense of humor and spending fun with each other. Playfulness and laughter can reduce stress, make happy memories, and strengthen bonds between people. Embracing humor in ordinary circumstances and avoiding overly serious thinking create a carefree and happy atmosphere. Laughing together, exchanging anecdotes, or playing games together helps maintain a lively and joyful connection.

In conclusion, long-term partnership success demands steady work, clear communication, empathy, mutual respect, trust, and shared experiences. Relationships can be robust and healthy if people practice active listening, showing appreciation, constructively handling conflict, encouraging one another's goals, and forgiving one another. A sense of humor and consistent quality time are also crucial for the happiness and resiliency of the partnership. These routines and behaviors contribute to developing strong, long-lasting bonds that improve general well-being and life satisfaction.

Continuous Learning

Ongoing education is essential when interacting with negative people because it gives them the information and abilities they need to manage difficult situations. Gaining knowledge about interpersonal dynamics, communication techniques, and psychological concepts facilitates the development of a more profound comprehension of maladaptive behaviors and the most effective means of addressing them. To stay resilient and promote favorable results, one must also be adaptable, or have the capacity to modify one's strategy in response to fresh knowledge and evolving conditions. This section examines the value of ongoing education and flexibility when interacting with unfavorable individuals, placing a focus on doable tactics for maintaining knowledge and adaptability.

The fact that lifelong learning improves emotional intelligence is one of the main reasons it's crucial while with negative people. Having emotional intelligence is essential for handling encounters with challenging people.

It encompasses self-awareness, self-regulation, empathy, and social skills. People can become more adept at comprehending, controlling, and empathizing with people by consistently studying about emotional intelligence. For example, engaging in emotional intelligence courses or reading books can offer insightful advice on maintaining composure under pressure, ultimately resulting in more positive outcomes.

Gaining a more profound comprehension of various personality types and behaviors is a crucial component of lifelong learning. Certain characteristics, such narcissism, passive-aggressiveness, or persistent whining, are frequently displayed by negative people. By becoming aware of them, people can create better coping mechanisms for certain characteristics. For instance, being aware of the traits of narcissistic behavior might assist someone in identifying manipulation and responding in a way that establishes boundaries. In a similar vein, becoming knowledgeable about passive-aggressive conduct can assist in recognizing mild indications of animosity and addressing them head-on before they worsen.

Keeping up with communication techniques is also crucial for handling negative people. Effective communication is the cornerstone of conflict resolution and the development of constructive relationships. This field of study requires ongoing learning of a variety of communication strategies, including nonverbal cues, assertiveness, and active listening. De-escalating confrontations and demonstrating empathy can be achieved by active listening, which entails giving full attention to what the other person is saying. People can learn how to set boundaries and communicate their demands without being aggressive or passive by participating in assertiveness training. People can minimize misunderstandings and negotiate relationships with negative people more skillfully if they regularly update their communication skills.

Another essential quality while interacting with negative people is adaptability. Unpredictable circumstances might arise when undesirable behavior occurs, and a one-size-fits-all strategy is rarely successful. Being flexible is being prepared to modify one's tactics in light of the particular situation and the other person's actions. For example, a tactic that suits a passive-aggressive coworker might not be appropriate for a friend who constantly complains. Being adaptable entails having an open mind to experimenting with many strategies and taking lessons from each one. This adaptability enables people to remain composed under different conditions and react to a broad variety of undesirable behaviors more skillfully.

Asking reliable sources for their opinions is a useful tactic for ongoing learning. Mentors, friends, relatives, and coworkers can offer insightful advice on how to deal with unfavorable people. They might see habits or behaviors that you are blind to and make helpful recommendations for how to get better. Seeking feedback regularly highlights the value of self-awareness in handling challenging situations and aids in identifying areas for improvement. Talking to others about these difficulties might also open your eyes to fresh ideas and approaches you may not have considered.

Taking advantage of professional development opportunities is another smart strategy to be knowledgeable and flexible. Numerous organizations provide training courses, workshops, and seminars for stress management, conflict resolution, and interpersonal skills. These courses offer organized learning opportunities that can improve your capacity to interact with unfavorable people. For instance, taking a conflict resolution workshop can teach you sophisticated methods for resolving conflicts and identifying points of agreement. Opportunities for professional growth also allow people to network with others who deal with comparable issues, promoting camaraderie and shared knowledge.

One of the best lifelong learning habits is reading books and articles about psychology, communication, and personal development. On these subjects, professionals who provide strategies and insights based on empirical facts have produced a plethora of material. Reading frequently keeps you updated on the newest findings and recommended practices while broadening your knowledge base. Books on positive psychology, for example, might offer strategies for preserving optimism and fostering resilience even in the face of negative individuals. Effective communication articles can provide advice on how to handle challenging conversations and enhance interpersonal relationships.

Continuous learning and flexibility also require self-reflection and mindfulness practices. Being mindful entails paying attention to your thoughts and feelings while stepping back from judgment. By using this technique, you can lessen the chance of reacting impulsively or reactively when interacting with negative people by being composed and focused. Self-reflection is assessing your relationships regularly, taking into account what worked and what could be improved. Keeping a journal will help you with this process by letting you record your experiences, reflect on your answers, and monitor your development over time.

To access more information and help, consider joining online forums or support groups specializing in handling challenging individuals. These organizations provide a forum for exchanging stories, asking for guidance, and picking up tips from others who deal with related issues. Engaging in dialogues and listening to diverse viewpoints can enhance your comprehension and offer helpful advice for handling undesirable conduct. Support groups provide affirmation and motivation, reassuring you that you are not the only one dealing with these difficulties.

In conclusion, handling negative individuals successfully requires constant learning and flexibility. People can manage difficult relationships more skillfully by developing their emotional intelligence, comprehending various personality types, honing their communication abilities, and being prepared to modify their plans of action depending on the situation. Seeking feedback, participating in professional development, reading pertinent literature, practicing mindfulness and self-reflection, and attending support groups are all valuable tactics for remaining knowledgeable and flexible. By making these efforts, people can improve their general well-being and level of life satisfaction by gaining the resilience and abilities necessary to control undesirable behavior and preserve healthy connections.

Personal Growth

Personal growth often arises from the most challenging situations we encounter, including challenging relationships. These connections can be highly motivating for personal growth even though they have the potential to be demanding and depleting. People can improve their coping mechanisms, build resilience, and increase their emotional intelligence by seeing difficult relationships as chances for personal development. This section explores how difficult relationships can be leveraged for personal growth, the skills and attributes that can be developed, and practical approaches to transforming adversity into positive change.

People are pushed out of their comfort zones and forced to face and resolve discomfort and conflict in challenging relationships. Resilience is the capacity to bounce back from setbacks and adjust to challenging circumstances, and this method can help develop these qualities. Being resilient is more than just enduring adversity; it also means coming out of it stronger and more competent. People can develop resilience while they are in a bad relationship by learning how to control their emotions, keep a positive mindset, and stay committed to their long-term objectives in the face of temporary setbacks. Managing a demanding boss, for example, can impart essential skills in persistence, stress reduction, and upholding professional integrity in stressful situations.

Tough relationships can also help develop emotional intelligence, another crucial aspect of human development, including social skills, empathy, self-awareness, and self-regulation. People frequently need to take a critical look at their feelings and responses when in difficult situations. The first step toward developing emotional intelligence is self-awareness, which helps people see how their emotions affect their behavior and why they feel the way they do. People can improve their ability to control their emotions and prevent impulsive reactions by reflecting on how they responded to difficult situations.

Testimonials also foster empathy, the capacity to comprehend and experience another person's emotions. People who are difficult to deal with frequently suffer with their own fears and insecurities, which can show themselves as difficult or unpleasant actions. People can grow more empathetic by attempting to comprehend the underlying causes of these actions. This is acknowledging the nuanced human feelings and experiences that underlie bad action rather than endorsing it. Increased empathy promotes compassion, strengthens bonds between people, and facilitates more peaceful dispute resolution.

Moreover, relationships that present challenges offer the chance to hone communication abilities. Healthy relationships and conflict management depend on effective communication. Conflictual situations frequently bring to light communication shortcomings in the areas of assertiveness, clarity, and active listening. Active listening entails paying close attention to what the other person is saying, empathetically reacting, and deliberately answering. Being assertive is properly and clearly communicating one's wants and boundaries without being aggressive or passive. People can improve their general communication skills and become more effective in both personal and professional situations by using these skills in difficult relationships.

Self-reflection is an effective technique for personal development, especially when handling difficult relationships. Finding patterns and opportunities for growth can be facilitated by pausing to reflect on encounters and think about the lessons that can be drawn from them. Journaling, meditation, or just dedicating some time to consider the past few experiences can all be part of this introspective practice. People can better understand their behavior, identify triggers, and create plans for dealing with similar circumstances by engaging in self-reflection. For instance, thinking back on a tense discussion with a family member can highlight more positive methods to interact and uncover underlying problems that need to be addressed.

The improvement of problem-solving abilities is a crucial component of personal development through difficult relationships. Complex problems in difficult relationships frequently call for careful consideration and original thinking to solve. By viewing these obstacles as chances to hone problem-solving techniques, people can improve their capacity to handle complex circumstances. This entails dissecting the issue, taking into account different viewpoints, coming up with a few possible remedies, and assessing the results. In both personal and professional spheres of life, problem-solving abilities are highly valued.

Another vital ability that can be developed during difficult relationships is setting boundaries. Boundaries safeguard a person's mental and emotional health by defining what constitutes appropriate behavior. Setting and enforcing boundaries is often necessary when dealing with problematic people in order to avoid being overburdened or taken advantage of. This process entails expressing one's boundaries clearly and consistently, as well as being prepared to leave circumstances if these boundaries are crossed. Gaining the capacity to establish sound limits strengthens one's sense of autonomy and self-respect.

Difficult relationships may present an opportunity to practice letting go and forgiving. Resentment and clinging to grudges can be emotionally taxing and prevent one from moving forward in life. To be able to forgive is to let go of the bad feelings that come with doing bad things, not to excuse bad behavior. This process can result from emotional release and an increased ability to empathize and comprehend. Forgiveness is a practice that facilitates moving past previous hurts and concentrating on one's own growth and beneficial relationships.

Furthermore, difficult relationships might inspire people to seek outside resources—like counseling, self-help books, or workshops—to better themselves. Expert assistance can offer priceless direction and resources for handling challenging situations and promoting personal development. Counselors can assist people in discovering underlying problems, creating coping mechanisms, and strengthening their resilience. Self-help books and seminars provide useful guidance and insights that can spur personal growth and enable people to manage difficult situations more skillfully.

In conclusion, even though they are sometimes demanding and stressful, hard relationships can present excellent chances for personal development. People can cultivate resilience, emotional intelligence, communication skills, self-reflection, problem-solving abilities, boundary-setting, and forgiveness by approaching these relationships with an attitude of learning and self-improvement. These abilities and qualities support overall achievement in both the personal and professional spheres in addition to helping to handle difficult situations. Accepting the chances and lessons of challenging relationships can result in significant personal growth and a more contented existence.

CHAPTER IX

Real-Life Applications

Workplace Scenarios

Successfully navigating the intricacies of working relationships is essential for both preserving one's personal wellbeing and attaining professional success. Managing challenging coworkers and superiors brings special difficulties that require communication abilities, emotional intelligence, and strategic problem-solving. This section examines several approaches to handling challenging relationships at work, stressing the significance of establishing boundaries, upholding professionalism, and looking for workable solutions.

Managing negative, competitive, and uncooperative behaviors is a common task when dealing with challenging coworkers. Being professional at all times is one of the first things to do in such scenarios. This entails controlling your emotions and reacting coolly and collectedly to provocations. You can prevent growing disagreements and set a model for professional behavior by not letting unpleasant coworkers upset your emotional balance. When a coworker says something snarky, for example, answering with something collected and impartial shows that you're a professional and helps to defuse the issue.

A further crucial strategy for handling challenging coworkers is effective communication. It is easier to resolve problems before they become more serious conflicts when there is clear, respectful, and direct communication. In this process, active listening is essential. You may foster mutual respect and understanding by paying close attention to what your colleague is saying, respecting their feelings, and thoughtfully replying. For instance, setting up a private meeting to address problems and discover common ground with a coworker who frequently criticizes your work might assist in clearing the air, enhancing communication, and mending strained working relationships.

Establishing limits is essential when interacting with challenging coworkers. Setting limits helps you develop appropriate conduct and safeguard your time and energy. By being clear and consistent about your limits, you can keep your coworkers from going too far and make sure that conversations stay civil and constructive. For example, suppose a coworker constantly brings up non-urgent issues during work hours. In that case, you can control disruptions and remain focused by gently but firmly asking them to set out a designated time for discussions. Enforcing these boundaries consistently serves to both establish and uphold their significance as well as foster a more orderly and courteous workplace.

Collaborating with demanding coworkers can be particularly tough, especially when their actions negatively impact team chemistry. In these situations, concentrating on shared duties and goals can assist in refocusing attention from individual disputes to group goals. A more cooperative environment can be fostered by highlighting the value of each member's contribution and teamwork. To promote togetherness and lessen conflict, for instance, highlighting accomplishments toward common objectives and praising individual efforts can be done at team meetings.

A distinct set of tactics is needed to deal with challenging employers because of the power dynamics at play. Having a tough employer can be difficult at times, especially when you must balance deference to their authority and standing up for your rights and boundaries. It's critical to always be professional because any hint of disdain or disobedience might make things worse. Instead of just letting feelings out, it's critical to approach confrontations with the goal of identifying solutions that all parties can agree on. For example, suppose your supervisor is micromanaging your work. In that case, you can constructively approach the issue by asking for a meeting to discuss your wish for more autonomy while highlighting your commitment to producing high-quality outcomes.

In handling a challenging relationship, it might also be helpful to understand your boss's point of view. Due to the intense pressure they frequently face to achieve corporate objectives, bosses can display challenging behaviors. Establishing rapport and fostering a more cooperative working relationship can be accomplished by exhibiting empathy and a readiness to comprehend their difficulties. One way to show your importance and dedication to the company is to acknowledge the pressures your supervisor is under and provide solutions that can lighten their burden or increase team productivity.

Establishing a foundation of trust and preventing misconceptions can be achieved by proactive and frequent contact with your supervisor. Keeping your supervisor up to date on your accomplishments, difficulties, and development guarantees that they are aware of your contributions and lessens the possibility of misunderstandings. Giving your supervisor regular status updates via meetings or written reports, for example, can assist to stay on top of things and handle any issues before they get out of hand. You can more successfully advocate for your needs and bargain for resources, support, or responsibility adjustments when you communicate clearly and consistently.

Documenting contacts and keeping track of essential communications and incidents is crucial when working with employers who are tough to work with. Should disagreements worsen or you need to ask upper management or human resources for assistance, this paperwork can greatly assist. You can have a precise and transparent record of events by taking thorough notes of meetings, emails, and instructions. This will give you a solid foundation on which to resolve problems or defend your decisions. For instance, keeping proof of your work and contributions on file can help refute unfair performance criticism from a boss and safeguard your reputation in the workplace.

In some situations, dealing with persistent problems with uncooperative coworkers or superiors may require requesting assistance from human resources (HR) or higher management. HR specialists can resolve disputes, offer advice on organizational policies, and suggest ways to improve the workplace. It's crucial to voice your problems to HR factually and professionally, concentrating on specific behaviors and how they affect your job rather than personal grievances. Documenting particular occurrences and their consequences on team morale and productivity, for example, can assist HR in determining the severity of the problem and take appropriate action if a colleague's behavior is creating a hostile work environment.

It is imperative to cultivate resilience and self-care habits to effectively handle the stress from challenging professional interactions. Having a positive outlook, creating useful coping mechanisms, and upholding a good work-life balance are all part of building resilience. Regular physical activity, mindfulness exercises, and asking friends and family for assistance can all aid in lowering stress and improving general well-being. You may better manage the emotional toll of challenging relationships and keep your attention and productivity at work by making self-care a priority.

In conclusion, managing challenging coworkers and superiors requires professionalism, clear communication, establishing boundaries, and resilience. People can handle complex working relationships more skillfully by remaining composed, encouraging candid communication, and concentrating on shared objectives. You can further improve your ability to manage conflicts and safeguard your professional well-being by getting support from HR or upper management, documenting encounters, and comprehending and empathizing with others' points of view. Practicing self-care and resilience can help you stay emotionally and psychologically strong enough to bear the strains of challenging relationships at work, eventually creating a more positive and productive work environment.

Family Dynamics

Managing negative relatives within family dynamics can be a particularly challenging and sensitive task, given the deep emotional ties and shared history involved. Family members' negative behavior can take many different forms, such as criticism, manipulation, passive-aggressiveness, and a general propensity to instigate conflict. It takes a combination of empathy, direct communication, boundary-setting, and self-care to manage these dynamics effectively. In order to preserve one's well-being and promote better connections, this section examines coping mechanisms for difficult family dynamics.

Recognizing the underlying causes of unfavorable relatives' conduct is the first step towards addressing them. Negative conduct frequently results from underlying problems like unfulfilled desires, envy, insecurity, or unresolved trauma. You can learn more about their potential motivations by empathizing with the problem. Recognizing that there might be more serious problems at hand rather than justifying negative behavior is what empathy is all about. A constantly judgmental relative, for instance, may be projecting their own fears or painful memories onto other people. Realizing this can assist in depersonalizing their actions and eliciting more sympathetic responses.

Having forceful and transparent communication is crucial while handling unfavorable relatives. Being honest about how you feel and what worries you can help to resolve problems before they get out of hand. It is crucial to express how their actions impact you using "I" phrases so as to avoid coming across as judgmental. Saying something like "I feel hurt when you make negative comments about my choices" emphasizes your emotions rather than the other person's actions. Reducing defensiveness and promoting more positive conversation are two benefits of this strategy. In these discussions, active listening is also quite essential. You can create an atmosphere that is more courteous and understanding by actually listening to your relative's point of view and respecting their emotions.

Establishing and upholding boundaries is one of the most critical tactics for handling dysfunctional family dynamics. Setting boundaries ensures that relationships stay civil and safeguards your emotional health. Be constant in upholding your boundaries and make sure they are understood. For example, you might respond, "I'm not comfortable discussing this topic," if a relative frequently brings up touchy subjects that upset you. Let's have a different conversation." If they continue, it's critical to firmly state your boundaries and, if needed, step away from the interaction. Enforcing limits consistently serves to both develop a healthier dynamic and to emphasize their relevance.

Restricting your interactions with toxic relatives could be important in some situations to safeguard your mental well-being. This is about cutting all connections; rather, it is about interacting less frequently or for shorter periods of time in order to reduce your exposure to negativity. For example, you may decide to see a family member less frequently or spend less time with them during family events if they are really draining. It's critical to put your health first and understand that keeping your distance from harmful conduct is acceptable. Managing expectations and averting confrontation can be achieved by politely expressing your need for space.

When coping with unsupportive relatives, getting help from other family members or friends can offer important perspective and emotional support. You can feel less alone and more equipped to handle the issue if you talk about your experiences and ask for guidance from trustworthy people. For instance, talking about your worries with a sympathetic cousin or sibling might foster understanding and a sense of support. They may also share knowledge or tactics that have helped them in comparable circumstances. A support system can also act as a cushion against the emotional damage that comes from unfavorable encounters.

Maintaining your emotional resilience when interacting with unfavorable relatives requires you to exercise self-care. Frequent self-care practices can help you feel better overall and minimize stress. These practices include exercise, meditation, writing, and hobbies. The fortitude required to manage difficult family dynamics can be obtained by setting aside time to rejuvenate and concentrate on enjoyable and soothing pursuits. For example, scheduling a daily quiet activity, like reading or taking a stroll, can help you decompress and lessen the effects of stressful situations.

When bad conduct is especially detrimental or persistent, it can be helpful to seek professional support. A therapist or counselor can give a safe environment to examine your feelings as well as tools and methods for handling challenging family relationships. You may strengthen your resilience, acquire better communication skills, and create healthier coping mechanisms with the aid of therapy. To increase confidence and efficacy, a therapist could, for instance, assist you in role-playing challenging talks or practicing setting limits. Getting professional assistance can also help you work through any underlying problems that might make dealing with unsupportive relatives more stressful.

Understanding that change is a slow process and that patience and persistence are necessary to manage negative family dynamics are key. Although you have no control over the acts of others, you do have power over how you react and how conversations go. Honoring minor accomplishments and advancements, such skillfully establishing limits or engaging in productive dialogue, can strengthen your endeavors and generate impetus for additional favorable transformations. Sustaining your efforts requires keeping an eye on the big picture and practicing self-compassion when faced with obstacles.

Having compassion and empathy for oneself is equally vital. Recognize the emotional strain of interacting with unsupportive family members and give yourself credit for the perseverance and effort needed. Treating yourself with the same consideration and compassion that you would extend to a friend in a comparable circumstance is the foundation of self-compassion practice. This can support a more positive self-image and lessen self-criticism, both of which are important for preserving your emotional well-being.

In conclusion, managing negative relatives within family dynamics involves understanding the root causes of their behavior, clear and assertive communication, setting and maintaining boundaries, and engaging in self-care. Asking for help from other friends, family members, or experts might offer more insight and support. Maintaining efforts to strengthen family ties requires self-compassion exercises and an understanding of the gradual nature of transformation. By implementing these techniques, people can safeguard their well-being, manage difficult family dynamics more skillfully, and promote happier, better relationships.

Social Interactions

Although it can be difficult, navigating social interactions with demanding friends and acquaintances is necessary for preserving one's wellbeing and harmonious relationships. To handle these relationships well, managers must frequently balance aggressiveness, empathy, and strategic communication. Friends and acquaintances who are challenging to get along with sometimes display negative, manipulative, inconsistent, or boundary-pushing tendencies. This section examines methods for interacting with these people, stressing the value of comprehension, open communication, establishing boundaries, and continuing self-care.

The first step in handling relationships with difficult friends and acquaintances is recognizing the underlying causes of their demanding conduct. Their actions frequently have deeper causes, such as unfulfilled desires, pain from the past, or insecurity. You can comprehend their point of view and react more empathetically if you approach these exchanges with empathy. Recognizing their emotions and experiences without necessarily endorsing their actions is a sign of empathy. For instance, a friend who is constantly negative may be dealing with personal problems that they find hard to express. Understanding this will enable you to take a more supportive stance toward the circumstance and depersonalize their actions.

When interacting with challenging friends and acquaintances, being firm and communicating clearly is imperative. Being honest about how you feel and what worries you can help to resolve problems before they get out of hand. Reducing defensiveness and promoting a more positive conversation can be achieved by using "I" statements to explain how their actions impact you. Saying something like "I feel hurt when you cancel our plans at the last minute" emphasizes you rather than the other person. This strategy promotes understanding and candid communication between parties. It's also crucial to actively listen, which is paying close attention to what the other person is saying and giving a considered response. It demonstrates your appreciation for their viewpoint and your sincere desire to find a solution.

Establishing and upholding boundaries is an essential tactic for handling challenging social situations. Setting boundaries ensures that relationships stay civil and safeguards your emotional health. Maintaining healthy relationships can be ensured by setting clear expectations for friends and acquaintances and being steadfast in upholding them. If a friend regularly makes harmful jokes about you, you could respond, "I don't find those jokes funny." Kindly put an end to producing them." If they persist, it's critical to establish your boundaries firmly and, if required, think about ending the relationship. Enforcing limits consistently serves to both develop a healthier dynamic and to emphasize their relevance.

It may occasionally be essential to cut off communication with challenging friends and acquaintances in order to safeguard your emotional well-being. This does not imply cutting all connections; rather, it suggests minimizing the amount of time or frequency of interactions in order to reduce exposure to negativity. For example, you may decide to see someone less frequently or spend less time with them at social events if they are a really exhausting acquaintance. It's critical to put your health first and understand that keeping your distance from harmful conduct is acceptable. Managing expectations and averting confrontation can be achieved by politely expressing your need for space.

While navigating challenging social situations, getting advice and emotional support from other friends or reliable people can be quite helpful. By talking to those who have been there before and asking for guidance, you might feel less alone and more in control of the relationship. For instance, talking about your worries with a buddy who is encouraging can foster understanding and a sense of unity. They may also share knowledge or tactics that have helped them in comparable circumstances. A support system can also act as a cushion against the emotional damage that comes from unfavorable encounters.

Maintaining your emotional resilience when interacting with challenging peers and acquaintances requires you to practice self-care. Frequent self-care practices can help you feel better overall and minimize stress. These practices include exercise, meditation, writing, and hobbies. The resilience required to manage difficult social dynamics can be obtained by setting aside time to rejuvenate and concentrate on enjoyable and soothing pursuits. For example, scheduling a daily quiet activity, like reading or taking a stroll, can help you decompress and lessen the effects of stressful situations.

When challenging conduct is really damaging or persistent, getting professional help may be helpful. A therapist or counselor can give a safe space to explore your feelings as well as techniques and resources for handling challenging social situations. You may strengthen your resilience, acquire better communication skills, and create healthier coping mechanisms with the aid of therapy. To increase confidence and efficacy, a therapist could, for instance, assist you in role-playing challenging talks or practicing setting limits. Getting professional assistance can also aid in the processing of any underlying problems that might be causing you tension while interacting with challenging friends and acquaintances.

Understanding that change happens gradually and that handling challenging social situations calls for perseverance and patience is crucial. Although you have no control over the acts of others, you do have power over how you react and how conversations go. Honoring minor accomplishments and advancements, such skillfully establishing limits or engaging in productive dialogue, can strengthen your endeavors and generate impetus for additional favorable transformations. Sustaining your efforts requires keeping an eye on the big picture and practicing self-compassion when faced with obstacles.

Having compassion and empathy for oneself is equally vital. Recognize the emotional strain of interacting with challenging friends and acquaintances, and give yourself credit for the perseverance and effort needed. Treating yourself with the same consideration and compassion that you would extend to a friend in a comparable circumstance is the foundation of self-compassion practice. This can support a more positive self-image and lessen self-criticism, both of which are important for preserving your emotional well-being.

In conclusion, effective social interaction management with challenging friends and acquaintances entails self-care, forceful and transparent communication, boundary-setting and maintenance, and an awareness of the underlying causes of their conduct. Consulting with friends or experts in the field can offer a different viewpoint and help. Maintaining attempts to enhance social interactions requires self-compassion exercises and understanding the gradual nature of change. Using these techniques, people can safeguard their well-being, create better, more positive relationships, and negotiate difficult social dynamics skillfully.

CONCLUSION

The book "Negativity Neutralized: A Guide to Handling Difficult People—Navigating Challenging Relationships with Grace" is a priceless tool for anyone looking to strengthen their interpersonal bonds and improve their general well-being via more skillfully handling negativity. The book gives a thorough framework for comprehending the intricacies of bad conduct and useful tactics for dealing with it positively. The main ideas and conclusions of the book are summarized in this conclusion, which also highlights their importance and possible influence on readers' lives.

"Negativity Neutralized" is based on the understanding that negative behavior frequently results from underlying problems like insecurity, trauma from the past, or unfulfilled needs. It is essential to grasp this to address challenging individuals with empathy and compassion as opposed to condemnation or rage. Readers are urged to see difficult encounters as chances for learning and development rather than as insurmountable challenges by recognizing the root reasons of bad behavior. This mental adjustment is essential to creating a more resilient and productive strategy for dealing with negativity.

The significance of proficient communication in handling challenging relationships is underscored in the book. It is emphasized that courteous, forceful, and transparent communication is essential for reducing tension and promoting understanding. Thorough exploration of strategies like "I" statements, active listening, and keeping a composed demeanor gives readers useful abilities that they can use in various situations. Readers may foster a culture where honest communication and respect for one another are valued by honing their communication skills, ultimately resulting in stronger and more fruitful interactions.

Establishing and upholding boundaries is yet another important topic in "Negativity Neutralized." Setting and maintaining boundaries is crucial for keeping one's mental and emotional health as well as the decorum of relationships. The book offers detailed instructions on recognizing inappropriate behavior, expressing boundaries clearly, and consistently upholding them. Readers may guarantee that their own needs and limits are respected and stop negative persons from going too far by setting and maintaining boundaries. This approach respects individual liberty and self-respect while also promoting healthier partnerships.

Throughout the novel, there are several references to emotional resilience. The capacity to maintain composure in the face of negativity is crucial for handling challenging situations without losing control or reacting irrationally. The book provides a number of methods, such as stress reduction, self-care, and mindfulness, for establishing and sustaining resilience. Readers may better tolerate the effects of negative behavior and keep a positive view, even in difficult times, by putting their well-being first and building resilience.

Personal development is presented as the primary result of putting the book's ideas into practice. The author challenges readers to see difficult relationships as chances for growth and development on a personal level. Readers can improve their communication, emotional intelligence, and general resilience through introspection and analysis of challenging exchanges. With the help of this growth mentality, obstacles can be turned into worthwhile learning opportunities, giving readers the confidence and efficacy to deal with negativity.

The significance of asking for assistance from others is also emphasized throughout the book. A support system, whether made up of friends, family, coworkers, or experts, can offer insightful viewpoints, counsel, and emotional affirmation. The author emphasizes the function of counselors and therapists in providing specific advice and strategies for handling challenging relationships. Seeking professional assistance can be very helpful in resolving ingrained problems and creating customized approaches to deal with negativity.

Furthermore, "Negativity Neutralized" offers a well-rounded strategy for handling negativity by fusing assertiveness with empathy. While assertiveness guarantees that one's needs and limits are respected, empathy aids in identifying the underlying causes of unwanted conduct. With the help of this dual strategy, readers may manage challenging situations with poise and firmness, promoting an atmosphere of respect and cooperation.

The book provides a planned personal action plan that incorporates its concepts into day-to-day living, which is a practical application. This approach calls for developing emotional resilience, practicing effective communication, setting and upholding boundaries, exercising empathy, and reflecting regularly in order to advance personally. Through adherence to this action plan, readers can implement the strategies in the book methodically and track their success over time. With this systematic approach, the ideas are guaranteed to become deeply embedded in their behavior, resulting in enduring improvements to their relationships.

All things considered, "Negativity Neutralized" is a thorough manual that gives readers the information and abilities they need to handle challenging relationships. Its focus on personal development, communication, limits, empathy, and resilience offers a comprehensive strategy for dealing with negativity. Using the book's concepts, individuals can convert difficult situations into chances for growth and learning, ultimately improving their well-being and cultivating more positive connections.

In conclusion, "Negativity Neutralized" offers a wealth of insights and practical strategies for dealing with difficult people and managing negativity with grace. A strong framework for managing difficult relationships is provided by the book's emphasis on comprehending the underlying causes of negative behavior, enhancing communication, setting boundaries, developing resilience, and encouraging personal growth. By adopting these ideas, readers can improve their ability to interact with others, safeguard their mental and emotional health, and foster a more upbeat and encouraging environment in both personal and professional settings. The book has the capacity to positively impact readers by teaching them how to deal with negativity, see obstacles as chances for personal development, and cultivate happier, more satisfying relationships.

Thank you for buying and reading/ listening to our book. If you found this book useful/ helpful please take a few minutes and leave a review on the platform where you purchased our book. Your feedback matters greatly to us.

9 798330 281077